# LIVING
*by*
# FAITH

## How the Impossible Becomes Possible With God

Dr AMANDA NICKSON

First published by Ultimate World Publishing 2020
Copyright © 2020 Amanda Nickson

ISBN

Paperback: 978-1-922497-64-2
Ebook: 978-1-922497-65-9

Amanda Nickson has asserted her rights under the Copyright, Designs and Patents Act 1988 to be identified as the author of this work. The information in this book is based on the author's experiences and opinions. The publisher specifically disclaims responsibility for any adverse consequences which may result from use of the information contained herein. Permission to use information has been sought by the author. Any breaches will be rectified in further editions of the book.

All rights reserved. No part of this publication may be reproduced, stored in or introduced into a retrieval system, or transmitted in any form, or by any means (electronic, mechanical, photocopying, recording or otherwise) without the prior written permission of the author. Any person who does any unauthorised act in relation to this publication may be liable to criminal prosecution and civil claims for damages. Enquiries should be made through the publisher.

**Cover design:** Ultimate World Publishing
**Layout and typesetting:** Ultimate World Publishing
**Editor:** Isabelle Russell
**Cover photo:** Amanda Nickson, The Camino Way, Spain

Ultimate World Publishing
Diamond Creek,
Victoria Australia 3089
www.writeabook.com.au

# Testimonials

"I have known Amanda Nickson since we were schoolgirls together. Amanda has the same qualities now that radiated from her then: a gentle spirit, a love for others, unwavering integrity and a comfort in her own skin. Amanda was a person I could rely on no matter what, and I still can. Living by Faith will captivate you because of the truth of its words. May Amanda's vulnerability help you in your faith journey or come to know Jesus, the Risen Lord, for yourself."
**Penny Mulvey, grateful friend, BA, MDS, GAICD, and Chief Communications Officer, Bible Society Australia**

"Most people, when they think about their preferred future, think in terms of positive outcomes and success in all aspects of life. This is good, but often the reality is that life can be somewhat brutal and unpredictable, and it takes a special kind of person to thrive rather than just survive. Amanda Nickson is that kind of person. As a long-term friend, I have observed her consistent faith carry her through crises of personal and family health, and general life challenges, while focusing on assisting others in crisis and completing

her PHD in Social Work. She has displayed an uncommon resilience, enabled by her deep and abiding faith in God."
    Rev. Peter Patterson, Pastor and Missionary

"In the many years I've known Amanda, her faith has remained unshaken regardless of what has transpired along her journey. As a cheery and authentic woman, she has always remained focused, purpose-driven, passionate, and unstoppable in her pursuit of God and his plans for her life, resulting in much influence on those that come in contact with her. It's this insight that she shares in her book, which I know will have profound depth, meaning and impact on those who read it."
    Nic Henry Jones, Director & Senior Digital Marketing Strategist, Market Me Marketing

"I see Amanda's faith in everything she does. It guides her every interaction and decision and consequently, she is a woman of integrity with a very clear moral compass. Amanda's professional vocation provides a perfect opportunity for her to show her service to others in action. I enjoy working with Amanda and value her commitment to her own self development and reflection.
    Jennifer Blackshaw, Director Organisational Services, Catholic Education Townsville

"Gotta love a good story… but Amanda Nickson's is a great story! A story of pure inspiration that certainly has gone the distance through challenges and strong faith. It is good that Amanda has been able to publish and retell rich events that we have keenly watched. But, by then inserting lessons learnt, this book invites others to join the journey and has moved from good to great!

*Amanda is an amazing person and it is a joy to walk some of the way beside her. Our lives are truly enriched. Thank you, Amanda, for your determination to grow and develop which is consistently displayed. You shine because you have learned lessons of life well beyond shallow facades. Thank you for allowing us the opportunity to watch, learn and emulate.*

**Peter Aspin, Pastor and Chaplain, and Jenny Aspin, Senior Teacher and author**


"Over the last 10 years, Mandy has been a prayer partner. We have prayed over each other's work issues, family issues and life in general. Through the steadfastness of our faith and the power of committing to prayer together, I've seen God move in astonishing and miraculous ways through our circumstances. Life isn't easy, but the journey is if you connect with someone like Mandy who will stand in the gap for you and with you and pray the prayer you are praying. Her own story of faith when staring down death, helping a young adult daughter through mental illness and navigating a reluctant teenager through school and into fulfilling adulthood, will inspire you to pray deeper, seek an earnest prayer partner and trust that your life is indeed in God's care."

**Bronwyn Cartledge, supply teacher**


"*Have you wondered what it means to live by faith?* Living by Faith *is one of the most inspiring real-life stories of an ordinary woman who dared to live by faith and in doing so, achieved extraordinary things in her life. Her story could well be yours if you dare to live by faith!*"

**Camillus De Almeida, Transformational Coach & Founder ViGEO Life and Leadership Development**

*"I have had the privilege of a long friendship with Amanda Nickson for over 40 years. Amanda has a strong Christian faith that has been the moral compass for her life. As a young adult, she looked to the Bible when making significant decisions about relationships. In more recent times she was an inspiration to me and to others, as she gave thanks to God for His protection when she incurred a significant injury which could have paralysed her, and then had to endure an arduous recovery program. Throughout her life she has faithfully endeavoured to grow in her understanding of God's majesty as He has revealed Himself through creation and through the Bible, and in faith she has endeavoured to be open to the Holy Spirit's transforming work in her life. Amanda continues to bring all areas of her life, personal, professional and academic, to God in prayer, dependent on a sure faith in Jesus as her Lord and Saviour."*

Phill Keefe, retired Managing Director

*"It has been encouraging to see how Amanda's faith has given her strength and warmth in the way she engages with others, tasks and challenges. She has been unfaltering in her faith when adversity struck and her relationship with God is a shining example for others. Her book will provide valuable insights about walking with the triune God and being blessed by his love."*

Dr Ines Zuchowski, Senior Lecturer, Social Work and Human Services, James Cook University

*"Faith has substance (Heb. 11) and it requires commitment and faithfulness. Amanda Nickson is like faith personified. Her faith in the Lord Jesus has seen her overcome obstacles, stretch her personal development, encourage others tremendously beyond themselves, blessing others with her wisdom and promoting God's*

*kingdom on earth. To know Amanda is to see faith and love at work and in action. I have been a witness to this for over 30 years and her book will share this faith with you."*

**Sheryl Place, former Chaplain,**
**Sarina State High School**

"*Social worker, academic and local church leader, Amanda Nickson explores themes such as prayer, compassion, servanthood, gratitude, transformation and hope in this inspiring book. As a long-term friend and colleague, I have watched Amanda face the nitty gritty of life's daily challenges with courage and determination, drawing on her deep well of faith. Throughout this book, Amanda shares personal stories of God's faithfulness from her own life's journey. If you want to develop the kind of faith that permeates all aspects of life, I can highly recommend this book.*"

**Dina Fyffe, Mentor, Coach, Community Mentoring**
**Program, Bridgeman Community Church**

# Dedication

To readers wanting to grow in their faith, and to be able to say: "I have fought the good fight, I have finished the race, I have kept the faith" (2 Timothy 4:7, New International Version).

# Contents

| | |
|---|---|
| Testimonials | iii |
| Dedication | ix |
| Introduction | xiii |
| Chapter 1: Miracle on Hinchinbrook | 1 |
| Chapter 2: You're going where? | 17 |
| Chapter 3: Lives saved in boating mishap | 27 |
| Chapter 4: Busy bees fly | 35 |
| Chapter 5: Throw me a lifeline | 43 |
| Chapter 6: Hang out with encouragers | 53 |
| Chapter 7: A mother's heart | 61 |
| Chapter 8: Creating your own Camino | 69 |
| Chapter 9: Walking for a cause | 79 |
| Chapter 10: Following your passion | 91 |
| Chapter 11: Gratitude | 97 |
| Chapter 12: Future focus | 103 |
| Afterword | 109 |
| About The Author | 111 |
| Acknowledgements | 113 |
| Speaker Bio | 115 |

# Introduction

Welcome to *Living by Faith*. This book is for anyone who is going through some struggles, challenges, or fears, and is wanting to find out how living by faith can make a difference. I certainly have had more than a few of these in my life.

It is also a book for Christians who want to be encouraged in their faith journey and anyone questioning whether God is real and relevant today. I decided to write the book because I wanted to share my experiences of knowing God and his miracles that are happening today to encourage others in their Christian faith and to share wisdom on the life of faith. Each chapter shares a principle of living by faith.

This book will provide inspiration, encouragement, and the keys to living a life of faith. Based on biblical principles, I was inspired to write this book after my miraculous survival of having a broken neck on a bushwalking trip and so many people telling me I was lucky. I don't believe in luck. I know it was God who protected me. Being able to share this story in this book will encourage others that God is here, and He is for us, not against us. This is the story I share in the first chapter which is looking at speaking aloud the Word of God and its power as a principle of faith. It demonstrates how the impossible can become possible with God.

After my broken neck, a few people said to me, "You should write a book". Then I thought about how much God has done for me in my life that I could share to encourage others in their faith. There have been many situations where I have witnessed God's hand over my life, even aside from the story of my broken neck. I was inspired to think about the keys behind many of the situations in my life where my faith has been stretched and then I have grown in faith. The following principles of faith unfolded across the chapters you're about to read:

- Chapter 1 - speaking aloud the Word of God and my miracle on Hinchinbrook Island
- Chapter 2 - hearing from God by telling the story of my interstate move from Sydney to Dysart, and how to get confirmation of what you have heard from God.
- Chapter 3 - prayer and what to do if you are prompted to pray for someone at a specific time.
- Chapter 4 - using your talents and provides background stories with musical events that unfolded.
- Chapter 5 - trusting God with some difficult and personal examples from my life.
- Chapter 6 - encouragement and how significant receiving encouragement can be in making it through challenging times.
- Chapter 7 - sharing your burdens and how powerful that is.
- Chapter 8 - the idea of self-compassion and how important looking after yourself is, including some of my experiences walking the Camino Way in Spain.

## Introduction

- Chapter 9 - showing compassion and helping others and what that does in you.
- Chapter 10 - re-inventing yourself or changing your story so that you can become who you want to be and follow your passions and dreams in life.
- Chapter 11 - gratitude and how being thankful can change your focus and thinking.
- Chapter 12 - asking God what your next step of faith is.

Throughout this book, I hope you are encouraged in your faith and come to believe that, with God, the impossible becomes possible.

## Chapter 1

# Miracle on Hinchinbrook

### Knowing and speaking aloud the Word of God

The Bible has been important to me ever since I decided that putting God first in my life and following Jesus was the only way to live a fulfilling life. God was the only sure thing and constant I could rely on in my life. As a child and teenager, I attended my local church and youth group and could see how different the youth leaders were to me, as they had a sense of joy, peace, and purpose. I wanted what they had. I sought out more information and made a very conscious decision to make Jesus the Lord of my life.

A couple of years later, when I was at university studying in my first year of a Bachelor of Social Work, I could choose an elective and I chose to study a subject on comparative religion. This helped me be more certain than ever that Christianity is definitely the one way to find and get close to God. I had confidence in undeniable, historical records, backing the miracles and claims of Christ. I wanted to be sure I was basing my life on truth. At this time, it became apparent to me how powerful the Word of God, the Bible, is.

Many different verses I have heard and read, and some I have memorised, amazingly spring into my mind at just the right moment in different situations in my life. God has a way of bringing to my remembrance the very words of life I need to know. Knowing and declaring (speaking aloud) the Word of God over my circumstances has been a key to successful living through all sorts of challenges and circumstances. In various situations, this key of knowing and speaking aloud a verse or verses from the Bible has paved the way to success and victory in the many challenges I have faced and has been life changing. Spending time reading and studying the Bible has been vital to my life in each and every day. This is how I can live by and walk by faith.

## Knowing and speaking aloud the Word of God (the Bible)

Firstly, why is it important to declare (speak aloud) the Word of God? The Word of God changes things, and we need to know the Word of God to do that. The Word of God is powerful, a living and active thing. "For the Word of God is alive and active. Sharper than any double-edged sword, it penetrates even to dividing soul and spirit, joints and marrow; it judges the thoughts and attitudes of the heart" (Hebrews 4:12, New International Version).

Don't underestimate the power of the Word of God!

# Miracle on Hinchinbrook

Secondly, miracles can happen just as they did in Bible times. Miracles do happen. Later in this chapter I will explain the miracle of protection that I experienced on a bushwalk on Hinchinbrook Island. It is my firsthand account of a miracle. The fact that I spoke aloud the Word of God at that time is, I believe, part of the miracle.

Thirdly, when we believe and speak the Word of God, it changes things. With God on your side, nothing is impossible, which we are reminded of when we read: "Jesus looked at them and said, 'With man this is impossible, but with God all things are possible" (Matthew 19:26, New International Version). There is a saying that "you and God are a majority".

Fourthly, there is power in the Word of God. You have the authority. You can speak to circumstances and they change. I am reminded of the story of the faith of the centurion in Matthew 8. This was a centurion whose servant was at home paralysed and in suffering. He asked Jesus to simply say the word for him to be healed, as he had a keen understanding of authority, and knew that Jesus simply needed to speak, not to come personally to his home. Jesus commended his faith (Matthew 8:5-10). Later, when talking to the disciples, Jesus said, "Because you have so little faith. Truly I tell you, if you have faith as small as a mustard seed, you can say to this mountain, 'Move from here to there,' and it will move. Nothing will be impossible for you" (Matthew 17:20, New International Version). So whatever mountain you are facing, it can be moved by faith! You can say to the mountain "move" and it will go. You will grow in your faith knowing this truth. Without faith, I am overcome by my problems. However, with faith and the Word of God as my guide, it makes all the difference.

One of my favourite verses that springs to mind often in times of difficulty in my life, is Philippians 4:13: "I can do all things through Christ who strengthens me" (New International Version).

Why "declare" the Word of God? The word declare means "speaking out with conviction and belief". The principle behind declaring the Word of God comes from the Bible itself. Think of the story of Jesus being tempted in the wilderness, where each time He answered, "It is written…", and He refuted the temptations of the Devil by speaking the scriptures (Matthew 4:1-11, New International Version). This is the example I draw on that shows me that there is great power and authority in the Word of God.

## My miracle experience on Hinchinbrook Island

What has been my experience of knowing and declaring the Word of God and seeing what it can do in my life? The Word of God has made a few huge differences in my life which I will illustrate with the following story – a true story of my real-life miracle on Hinchinbrook Island.

I will start with the unusual phone call I received on my mobile phone from my doctor in June 2010. His words kept going through my head. He said to me, "Where are you?" I answered, "Outside the X-ray place." He said, "Go straight to Emergency. You have an unstable neck fracture. Do not look down, do not look sideways, go straight there." I said "Okay". I kept thinking, "He must be wrong. I couldn't possibly have a fracture, could I? This sounds serious, very serious. How could this be right?"

It all started with a bushwalking trip a week earlier. It had been with great anticipation, after months of planning, the long-anticipated trip to Hinchinbrook Island had begun. With my husband Daryl, and friends Wendy, David, Lyn and Phil, we hopped into the minibus and headed from Townsville in North Queensland to Lucinda, where a boat was waiting to take us across the Hinchinbrook Channel to the southern end of Hinchinbrook Island. The 32-kilometre walk of the famous Thorsborne trail awaited. We had decided to do the track from South to North over five days.

The start of the walk, Hinchinbrook Island, Queensland, 2010

The trip had taken shape about a year before as a way for three couples to have a fun camping and hiking holiday together whilst seeing a truly magnificent wilderness area. It also acted as motivation to work towards getting fit with this hike as a goal. We had coordinated holidays, flights, buses, and boats. We had carefully planned and weighed all the gear in our backpacks, including meals with dehydrated foods and walking poles purchased to help with the expected steep sections of the hike. The trail along Hinchinbrook's east coast is recommended for fit and experienced bushwalkers only. It is not a graded or hardened walking track and often, it is rough and difficult to traverse. We were all experienced bush walkers.

On arriving at George Point, that afternoon we had a short 7.5-kilometre walk along the beach, across creeks and through scrubland to our camping spot for the night at Mulligan Falls. We set up camp and had a dip in the stream to cool off. It was clear water and very refreshing. The adventure had begun.

On day two we made an early start. We had climbed up a rocky section of track that was very steep that had a chain attached to the rocks so that you could pull yourself up or hold on going down. The track followed a creek. Meandering up and down, following the track, we came to a section where I looked down and thought, wow- this is steep, where can I put my feet here? Before I had time to think any more, I was tumbling down the steep section of track, head over heels. My backpack had changed my centre of gravity, and I felt like I was almost being pushed down the track when I looked down. I landed on my back about three or four metres down the track with my right arm jammed against some rocks. Daryl and the others rushed down to see if I was alright and somehow, helped me walk a few more metres down to the creek where I lay down on some large rocks to recover while my friends assessed whether or not I could keep going. I was rather shaken.

## Miracle on Hinchinbrook

My legs were fine. My right arm seemed limp and I had two numb fingers (pins and needles) on my right hand. My neck seemed a little numb and tingly but alright. I thought I must have done something to my arm or elbow that was affecting my hand. Phil kindly boiled a billy so that I could have a cup of tea – my friends knew me well! After resting for quite a while, I finally thought I was okay to go on. I didn't seem to have anything broken or life threatening. Daryl took my pack for the rest of the day. We kept going to Zoe Falls where we set up camp in a beautiful, designated spot, just off the beach, tucked in behind some trees. I was trying not to use my right arm. It was weak and kept giving way if I attempted to rely on it for balance, so I put on a sling to remind myself not to.

The next day we had planned a rest day, and I was very glad for it. My neck was sore, and I was finding it hard to bend my head down. I started using one hand placed under my chin to prop up my head– my own portable neck brace!

Day four was the longest day of the hike. It was the 12.5-kilometre section from Zoe Falls to Nina Bay, passing Little Ramsay Bay. The guidebook suggested eight hours was needed to walk this distance, as it had a number of creek crossings and rock hopping sections. I was concerned. I would have to carry my own 14-kilogram pack for the day. We made our way through a swamp where it was difficult to find the track. We searched for and followed the markers. That day was a challenge! My neck was very sore. I walked with Daryl, crying, and said, "I can't do this". He said, "Yes, you can", and he prayed for me. The others had gone ahead of us as I was even slower than usual.

Later the track followed a creek bed, which was dry in parts and not in others. It was a rock-hopping nightmare, with rocks large and small everywhere. Some rocks you would hop onto and they

# Living by Faith

**Walking with the sling with my limp arm
and with an unstable neck fracture**

would move. This happened several times and at one point I ended up overbalancing and landed on my bottom. I sat there crying, thinking, I can't do this. I sat there for quite a while, thinking what it meant if I really couldn't do this. A rescue team would have to walk in for days to reach me. There was no phone reception. This was a remote area on a remote island. It sounded too dramatic. Then I remembered a verse from the Bible: "I can do all things through

Christ who strengthens me" (Philippians 4:13, New International Version). I started saying this aloud and declared this over my situation. I asked God to help me. I got up and continued walking from rock to rock. I stated out loud, "I can do all things through Christ who strengthens me", and would take one step. I repeated the words and took another step. I acted brave and bold, even though I wasn't feeling much of either. Some 10 hours later, I finally made it to camp with Daryl just before dusk.

I was totally exhausted. I waited while Daryl put up the tent and then immediately lay down in it. My friends took my turn for cooking dinner. I was so grateful. I would have skipped dinner and stayed resting in the tent all night, but I remembered it was Daryl's birthday. I got up to retrieve the section of fruitcake I had carefully baked and packed in my billycan as the surprise birthday cake for dessert that night.

My neck did not like it when I looked down. I had used up all the Panadol available in my first aid kit and my neck was complaining. With a stroke of brilliance, I asked the others, "Does anyone have some spare Panadol?" Everyone pooled their first aid supplies of Panadol so I was able to take them continuously every four hours. I was extremely grateful that everyone had packed some just in case!

The spectacular scenery and pristine beaches were in the background. The next day, all of us walked the four kilometres to Ramsay Bay. Dave and Wendy were staying another night on the island. Lyn, Phil, Daryl, and I met the boat to leave the island and travel to Cardwell. Lyn mentioned to the crew on the boat that I had a sore neck, and they produced a hot pack which I applied - what bliss!

We settled into the accommodation we had booked that night in Cardwell. We had only been able to book a return minibus to

Townsville for the next day. I enjoyed a hot shower after camping for five days. I decided to walk to an ambulance station I had seen earlier up the road. I explained to the ambulance officer that I had fallen while bushwalking on Hinchinbrook Island and had a sore neck and was worried about the minibus trip home to Townsville the next day. I asked if there might be a neck brace I could have to use on the trip. The ambulance officer said they did not have any. He suggested I use hot and cold packs and that I could use a towel wrapped around my neck or a folded newspaper to make a brace for the trip. He also suggested that I could go to Ingham Hospital for an X-ray if I wanted. Not having a vehicle and not knowing how I could travel to Ingham from Cardwell and back in time for our bus trip back, I thought I would wait until I got home to Townsville and see my local doctor the next day. I rang and booked an appointment for the following afternoon with my GP.

Not having hot or cold packs handy, as I had been bushwalking on an island, I went to the local supermarket. The closest thing I could find was a hot water bottle and some esky bricks. I bought those. I used the hot water bottle straight away and put the esky bricks in the freezer.

The next day I used my towel as a neck brace and the hot water bottle as a shock absorber as we travelled home by minibus, the bumpy and often pot-holed Bruce Highway. Soon after getting home, it was time for the doctor's appointment. I was in a lot of pain and thought I might have slipped a disc or pulled some muscles. Phil drove me to the doctor as I did not want drive as I did not want to turn my head which I would need to do if I drove. The doctor referred me for an X-ray, and Phil dropped me off. Before I got back to the doctor's surgery, my mobile phone rang. I remember very distinctly what the doctor said to me. He said, "Amanda, where are you? Go straight to Emergency. You have an unstable neck fracture.

Do not look down, do not look sideways – go straight there. They will stabilise it for you."

I thought, that can't be right! I have been walking for days, tripping and slipping. They must be going to give me a neck brace or something and then I'll go home. My friends took me to the hospital. Arriving in Emergency five days after my fall on Hinchinbrook Island seemed surreal. How could this be an emergency? I expected that I would soon be phoning my friends to come and pick me up. I was wrong. I was fitted with a hard neck brace (collar) which had

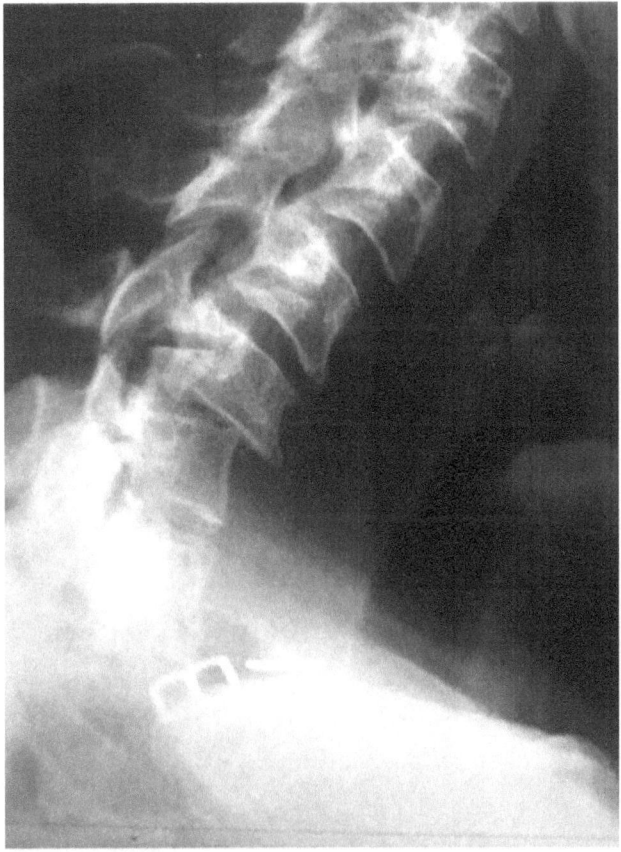

X-ray. Neck fracture at C6 and C7.

metal sections to stop any movement in my neck. I was cut out of my t-shirt as the staff did not want to move my neck at all. I was required to have scans, MRIs, and then discussions about possible surgery, possible traction or a halo brace were suggested.

I had fractured my C6 vertebrae and I had badly damaged a disc between my C6 and C7. The disc was totally squashed. My neck was also dislocated and the vertebrae at C6 and C7 seemed to be sitting at a strange angle to each other. Upon being assessed by neurosurgeons, I was advised that this was a serious spinal injury.

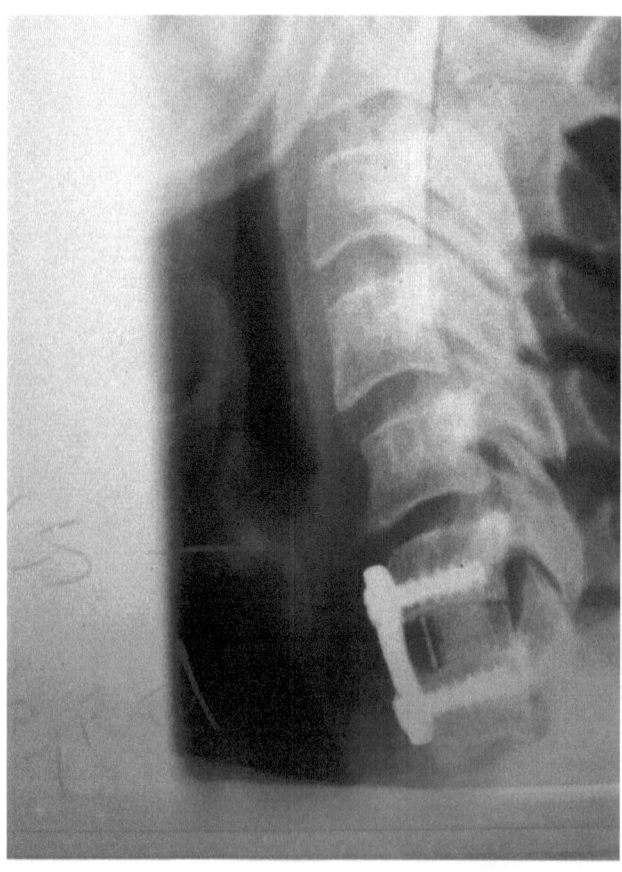

X-ray, titanium plate, screws and spacer after surgery

## Miracle on Hinchinbrook

I remember wondering how it was that I was alive and walking if I had suffered such a serious spinal injury.

I had surgery two days later, a week after my fall. The disc between C6 and C7 was removed and replaced by a spacer. I had a titanium plate screwed to these two vertebrae to hold my neck straight. A halo brace was also put on, which I would wear for the next thirteen and a half weeks! This is a contraption that has four screws that are screwed into your skull, two at the front into your forehead, and two at the back. These were tightened each week, so a weekly trip to the hospital clinic was needed.

So many people made comments about how "lucky" I was not to be paralysed, and that I was not a paraplegic or quadriplegic! Doctors, nurses, and friends were amazed that I had kept going on the hike, for another four days. I don't believe in luck. I knew God had looked after me on Hinchinbrook. What a miracle that any of the innumerable trips and stumbles I had walking those twenty odd kilometres after my fall with an unstable neck fracture had not caused my spinal cord to break!! The miracle was that I was walking and made it off the island - not seriously and permanently disabled. I hadn't died! Many people die from broken necks.

Would you consider allowing a person with an unstable neck fracture to hike a difficult bush track in a remote wilderness area, carrying a 14-kilogram pack, over rocks and boulders, crossing creeks and swamps, for four days and the fracture not move or worsen? It is hard to comprehend. I have thought God must have had angels working overtime holding my head up and supporting me. He must have more for me to do! My time is not up on this earth!

Recovery with the halo brace was challenging. I couldn't drive for three and half months, and bathing was a challenge. I have made

**Amanda in the halo brace**

a full recovery. I still have two fingers with pins and needles, but I am able to use the computer and play piano. I think of the pins and needles as my daily reminder that I am a walking miracle. I give all glory to God for protecting me for His purposes. I am forever grateful.

## What ifs

You might be thinking that it's all very well to use the Word of God if you know it well, but what if you don't know the Bible? You can look up relevant verses by topic, you can start reading and studying the Bible. God can bring to your remembrance verses when needed. There are many resources available to assist you in studying the Bible. Some further resources are at the end of this chapter and at the end of this book.

What if I don't have enough faith? All you need is faith the size of a mustard seed. Have you seen mustard seeds? They are tiny!

What if this saying aloud and declaring the Word of God doesn't work? I say, what if it does? You don't know unless you try. What have you got to lose? Give it a go.

# Living by Faith

## Three actions you can take as a result of reading this chapter

1. Decide to read the Word, the Bible. Study it – become familiar with key verses.

2. Decide to declare the word, and then declare the Word of God over your circumstances.

3. Expect there to be changes. Expect those mountains to move. Pray with faith!

**Additional information and resources**

To search for verses by topic or reference, see: https://www.biblegateway.com/

Also, https://www.youversion.com/ has a Bible App with a huge number of reading plans on different topics

To view a video of my story about my miracle on Hinchinbrook Island, you can view me telling the story at https://www.youtube.com/watch?v=vclla-Q9Z9E

A copy of this chapter is available as a pdf for free from my website: http://www.amandanickson.com.au/ if you would like to pass this good news on to others who may be interested.

More offers can be found at the end of the book.

*Chapter 2*

# You're going where?
## Hearing from God

I had just resigned from a permanent community development job with the Baulkham Hills Shire Council in Sydney to move to Dysart in Queensland. And my boss said to me, "You're going... where?"

Before I tell you more about that story, let me tell you about why hearing from God is so important. Hearing from God is essential because being in the will of God and fulfilling the call and purpose of our life brings fulfillment, peace, and joy. I want to be in the will of God. Secondly, having an assurance of our direction and receiving confirmation from God makes those big decisions easier to make and may not be as hard as you think.

Recognising God's voice and following his leading comes from knowing God through our relationship with him. This is developed in our times spent in prayer, studying the Word of God and in worship, where we get to know His voice.

Confirmation is also helpful. How we can hear from God can come in different ways, whether that's from reading the Word of God where a particular passage or verse "speaks" to you (that is God speaking to you through his Word), a meeting with someone who might be someone you look up to in their walk with God, a Pastor or church leader, who is wise in the things of God or with another Christian or person at what I call a "God appointment" or "God-incidence" (I do not believe in "coincidences", only "God-incidences").

How have I heard from God? In my life there have been many divine appointments where I've met with someone that I have later thought, wow, how did God arrange that? I have also heard the still, small voice of God when I am praying quietly and reading the Bible.

What have you got to do when seeking to hear from God? It can be a small step of faith that leads into big things in God. Do you ever think about what God has in store for you? He is a good, good father who wants to give good things to his children.

If you have ever been at the crossroads of a big decision, you know that taking no action is a decision and an action. Moving forward with steps of faith involves action. As a result of a huge decision for me, to leave Sydney and move to Dysart in Central Queensland to be closer to a man I thought I loved and wanted to get to know more, I have ended up married for over 35 years and have three wonderful children who wouldn't be here if I hadn't taken that first step of faith and heard from God.

An interesting fact is that it is easier to change direction if we are already moving. If we are starting from a stopped position it is harder. Think about a car. If it is stationary and you are having to push start it, that is very hard work. If the car is already moving, you can easily change direction by just touching the steering wheel.

So, what are the ways that we can receive confirmation from God or hear from God?

Seeking counsel from godly people in our lives can confirm or stop a decision. We can pray and seek God ourselves. We can look in the scriptures and see if what we're thinking of lines up with the Word of God. God would never ask us to do something that is outside of what is in the Bible. We can seek to hear God's confirmation as a still small voice. The Bible says that faith comes through hearing and hearing from the Word of God. I believe hearing from God is hearing from the Word of God. Can you take small steps in your planning? Sometimes God's plans may not receive the praise of the world's wisdom, which leads me to my story about the question I had from my boss.

He asked me, "You're going... where?" I answered, "Dysart".

The story started five months earlier when I had been on a holiday with a girlfriend, Liz, who I knew from university. We both enjoyed bushwalking and rainforests and had been camping on Fraser Island. It was whilst on holidays there that we met a very nice man, Daryl, who later became my husband. Liz and I had been walking up a beach for miles with the purpose of getting to Eli Creek. This creek is famous for being crystal clear and having rainforest growing from its banks. We saw a minibus approaching and decided to see if we could hitch a ride up to this creek. I have never hitch-hiked before, or since – it is not something I would normally do! The minibus stopped and gave us a lift further up the beach to the creek.

On the bus there were several young people, and we started chatting. One fellow, named Daryl, seemed very nice. He had come to the Island to get away from his work in the Department of Primary Industries in Emerald and wanted this time away to study the Bible. He was doing some Bible College course and had come up to see this creek as a break from his studies. I thought, that is interesting. Daryl is a Christian. Later that day, Daryl went back to where he was staying, and my girlfriend and I went back to where we were camped.

The next day is when one of these God- incidences happened. Liz and I had been camping on the beach and our tent was located behind a sand dune not visible from the beach. We decided to stand up and have a look at the beach and climbed up to the top of the sand dune. Just at that exact moment in time, Daryl was riding past on his motorcycle, looking for us. It was God's timing and arrangement, not a co-incidence. A "God-incidence". He saw us and came and chatted to us. I had distracted him from his studies!

We spoke a bit more. The three of us went to a campsite where we met a family and some other campers. It became apparent that Daryl was a Christian who was active in sharing his faith with the people around him, including the other campers we had just met. Liz and I were also talking about our Christian faith. I thought, oh, that's great. Daryl has always been someone who is keen to share his Christian faith, just like me.

Fast forward a few more walks and talks and Daryl and I discovered, on the night before I was to return to Sydney, that we both thought that we were in love with each other and were hoping and believing it could be God's will for us to be together as husband and wife, down the track. Daryl made it clear that his future could include being in ministry. I said that was fine with me because I also felt I had a calling to minister to people in rural Australia.

## You're going where?

I reviewed living in Sydney as Daryl was living in Emerald in Central Queensland. We had been having a long-distance romance for about six weeks. In those days with no email, no zoom, or Facebook, face time or skype, it was a weekly phone call and writing letters that we were sending to each other every few days. We were hearing about what God was doing in each of our lives. Daryl was very involved with the Emerald Assembly of God Church. I decided I would look in the newspaper and see if there was a social work job I could find somewhere in Queensland, even if it was in Brisbane, that would be a lot closer than Sydney. I wanted to get to know Daryl and the church he attended more.

The very first weekend I looked in the newspaper, the Sydney Morning Herald, I saw a job for a child protection social worker in a town named Dysart, which I had never heard of, but the advertisement said it was three and a half hours northwest of Rockhampton. I knew that Daryl was living in Emerald and that was three hours West of Rockhampton. I thought, wow, what are the chances of that? The very weekend I looked for a job and there is one actually close to where Daryl is living. In a neighbouring town! I applied for the job, but in the meantime, Daryl decided to visit me in Sydney. Another amazing "God-incidence," not coincidence, is about to happen.

At that time. I was looking for a church where I would feel more at home. I had grown up in the Presbyterian Church, which became the Uniting Church. I had stopped going for a while because I was looking for something more or different in church. When Daryl visited Sydney, we decided to visit a church I'd heard about, but had never been to, called Telopea Baptists. We travelled there and found the building which had a very large group of people, probably several hundred, gathered for the morning service. As we sat down, Daryl started chatting to the person sitting next to him. That does not sound that exciting, however, what was remarkable was who this woman was. She was from Queensland. She was from Central Queensland. In fact, she was from Dysart and had just left a job there. It turned out that she had just resigned from the very job that I was applying for! What were the chances of that? Randomly sitting next to this person in that crowded church! It was another God-appointment, not a coincidence! I took that as a confirmation from God that I was on the right track in applying for that job.

I had the job interview in Brisbane and was successful and was appointed as a Supervisor with the Department of Children's Services, as it was then, in the town of Dysart. The role serviced several surrounding towns including Clermont, Capella, Moranbah, Tieri and Middlemount. Daryl continued to live in Emerald, which was an hour and a half by road from Dysart. I lived in Dysart during the working week and travelled to Emerald most weekends, staying with different friends I made through the church. Daryl proposed to me in Townsville a fortnight before I moved to Dysart to commence my role with Children's Services. We had visited his family in Townsville and had a short holiday before starting my new job. I was engaged to a Queenslander I had met five months earlier.

That was the beginning of my story of moving from Sydney to Dysart. We were married the following year, six months after we became engaged, and married having known each other for only 11 months.

Another step in me seeking confirmation of my move inter-state was to speak to my mother. I loved and respected her immensely and I wanted to know her views, even though I was really worried about asking her. What would I do if she encouraged me not to go? I spoke to her about the job opportunity in Dysart and how I thought I loved this Daryl I had met. And she was very encouraging from a professional point of view. She said there would be nothing lost. Even if my relationship with Daryl didn't progress, she suggested

## You're going where?

that professionally moving to a different region, being able to work in a different field within social work was all good experience that could be added to my resume and that nothing would be wasted. So that gave me another level of assurance that I could move with my mother's blessing inter-state.

I recalled that I had always a desire placed on my heart to serve and be in country areas of Australia. I saw that this was one way that I could do that, serving not only in my job, but also in a church, in a rural area. It was like God was answering the prayers that I had in my heart for a long time.

Wedding, Amanda and Daryl, 6 April 1985

Another example of hearing from God was another time I was looking at changing jobs. I really wanted to hear from God. And that was when I had been in a permanent social work position with a federal government department as a senior social worker with Centrelink. I was becoming very exhausted and almost burnt out from crisis intervention work. I was looking at doing some study and had enrolled to do a PhD at James Cook University (JCU). The very first day I went to JCU to start working on my PhD, the Head of Department, Jane, came to see me unexpectedly and asked, "Would you like to work in the department doing the Field Education Coordinator position?" She could offer me a part time contract for six months but couldn't guarantee anything beyond that.

Jane needed a decision fairly quickly. I just felt in my heart that this was where God wanted me to be. He was opening the door to a new area. I spent overnight praying and seeking God, and I really believed this was where God wanted me to be. It might have looked foolish because I was leaving a permanent full-time position, but in God's economy, I just knew this is where he wanted me to be. I did speak to my permanent employer and asked, could I take leave without pay with the option to go back after six months thinking if there was no further contract with James Cook University, I would still have a job. However, this employer did not approve my request for leave without pay, saying I either had to resign straight away or return to the workplace. So, in another step of faith, I resigned my permanent job and took up a part time contract for six months, because there was just so much opportunity there for me at James Cook University. I believed that this was a God appointment. This opened the door to me becoming a lecturer for the next 13 years.

Whilst I had a number of part-time contracts initially, and then full-time contracts, I eventually got a permanent full-time position and believed I was in the place God wanted to me to be for a season.

A couple of years earlier, I had unsuccessfully applied for a job at James Cook University. It had been my desire and on my heart to go there for some time.

## What if we get it wrong?

I have often thought, but what if I made the wrong decision or go in the wrong direction? We can always learn from our mistakes. And I believe with God, nothing is wasted. Every experience I have had, even hard times and tough times, has added to building my character and given me greater empathy with others in challenging situations. I think there is really nothing to lose when we step out in God's will and take a step of faith.

## Three actions you can take as a result of reading this chapter

What are three actions the reader can take as a result of reading this chapter?

1. What is a decision you want to hear from God about?

2. What is a way you could seek confirmation of your decision? Who could you speak to about it? and

3. When is a time you can spend praying, reading the word and seeking God about this decision, and then make a plan?

## Additional information and resources

Ways to read and apply the Word of God:
The S.O.A.P. method (using the acronym SOAP) (reference: https://lovegodgreatly.com/how-to-soap/
Scripture – Read the Scripture (Bible verses)
Observation – What is God saying to you in this verse?
Application – How can you apply this in your life?
Prayer – Pray about it.

*Chapter 3*

# Lives saved in boating mishap
## Prayer

The headline on the front page of the Townsville Bulletin said, "Mobile phone saves family", but I knew it was God who had saved them. God had answered my prayers, like he had so many others'.

**Why do we pray?**

Firstly, because prayer changes things. Prayer is having a conversation with the God of creation, who loves us, and wants the best for us. He has the power to intervene in circumstances and change outcomes and situations.

Secondly, to build our relationship with God, we need to spend time connecting with him. To get to know someone, you spend time talking with that person and listening to them talking with you. How can we get to know God and hear from God if we don't spend time with Him and know His voice, how can we hear from Him? By spending time praying.

Thirdly, if you are prompted to pray, pray. Soon, I will give an example of this regarding my husband and two daughters in a boating mishap. Sometimes God brings to our mind different people. When this happens, I always pray for them. It is often God's timing for prayer in a situation of need or danger.

Fourthly, God wants us to pray. The Bible commands that we are to pray without ceasing.

Fifthly, answered prayers are a testimony. When a prayer is answered, that can be a great encouragement to us, to our faith and to others who may be praying and believing for their breakthrough and miracle. Sometimes answers come quickly, sometimes, answers may take years.

What does the Bible say about prayer? "You do not have, because you do not ask God" (James 4:2, New International Version), and "But when you ask, you must believe and not doubt" (James 1:6, New International Version). These are reminders that I need to ask and pray with faith.

God knows our needs before we ask. The Bible asks us to pray without ceasing. That is because God wants to have a relationship with us. He wants us to bring our thoughts and concerns, our burdens, our worries to him.

## Lives saved in boating mishap

What is prayer? Prayer is simply talking to God. Talking and communicating are how we build our relationships with other people. It is the same with God. The Bible teaches us to pray with thanksgiving, giving thanks in all circumstances. Are we praying with expectation? Are we praying and speaking with authority?

Prayer has made a huge difference in my life. Here are some very memorable examples. The first story is regarding a boat rescue story, where I heard very specifically from God. I had an urgent prompting to pray for the safety of Daryl and my two daughters.

My husband and I, and our three children who at that time were eight, five, and two years old, had been camping for a couple of nights on Goold Island, which is just east of Cardwell, North of Hinchinbrook Island in North Queensland. Goold Island National Park is approximately 17 kilometres from the coast. We had come to the end of a lovely camping holiday on this small island which the children had enjoyed. We had spent time looking at starfish on the beach and had found goannas in the trees. We had travelled to the island in two different boats. The children and I came on a ferry that dropped us off at the island. The ferry was very strict on how much luggage you were allowed to have per person and limited what it allowed you to take. It was strongly encouraged that camping gear must be taken in a separate boat. Daryl brought our small dingy with all the camping gear to the Island. The return date and time for the ferry had been arranged and the day came to return home.

The girls decided to go with Daryl on the dingy which was loaded with the camping gear. They all had their life jackets on. The ocean had seemed calm when they set off from the island ahead of me in the early afternoon. I was waiting for the ferry with my young son, Tim. I was just sitting, reading, waiting quietly with my son for the ferry later in the afternoon and I had this definite prompting from the Holy spirit to pray for Daryl and the girls. And I thought, oh, that's odd. I don't often get direct promptings from the Holy Spirit or often feel that God is talking to me directly to do something urgently, straight away. So, I questioned it. But it was clear. I heard, "Pray for their safety, pray for them now." So, I did! I spent the next hour praying fervently for their safety, for their protection. I had no idea what had happened, but God was telling me to pray for them. So, I kept praying.

Finally, the ferry arrived. Tim and I had no sooner boarded the ferry when straight away, the captain of the ferry was asking me a lot of questions about Daryl and his boat. "Can you describe it? What colour is it? Do you know the registration number?" I said, "Oh, it's just a small dingy. It's a silver metal colour. I don't know its registration number." He explained that there had been a report of an upturned boat and that the police, the National Parks vessel, and the coast guard volunteers were all searching for my husband's boat and my children! The ferry was keeping an eye out for it as well. You can imagine my anxiety at this point in time! I was praying even more on the ferry as we travelled back to Cardwell.

Finally, I got to the jetty in Cardwell and waiting on the jetty were lined up an ambulance, the fire brigade, the local police and the local newspaper. Everyone was waiting for Daryl and the girls who had been found by this time by a National Parks vessel. Apparently, the police had been about to phone for an emergency helicopter to join the search when they were found. The paramedics checked over the girls who had slight hypothermia but were otherwise unharmed. They had been in the water for over an hour. An unexpected wave swamped and overturned the boat. Daryl had stored a mobile phone in a plastic lunch box in the boat and was able to grab this and miraculously had been able to phone triple zero from the mobile phone and got through

## Lives saved in boating mishap

before the battery had run out. The people doing the rescue told me that looking for such a small boat which had been upturned in a stretch of 17 kilometres of water was like looking for a needle in a haystack. Impossible. They also told me that Hinchinbrook Channel in that area was known as "shark gully". I was very glad I had not known this information earlier!

I was so thankful that my family were okay, and I give God all the glory. It was quite an experience. All of the camping gear is on the bottom of the Hinchinbrook Channel. Some items went floating past Daryl. Those things do not matter. The important and main thing is that God protected the lives of my loved ones! I had been given that opportunity to pray for their safety and protection. Daryl had also been praying! We were both so thankful that God had made a way for them to be found when, as I have found over and over with God – He makes a way. When it is impossible for man, God makes it possible.

After the boat rescue, we were contacted by media outlets, local television stations and the local newspaper because the rescue situation had highlighted a gap in mobile phone coverage in the region. Apparently when the boats had been looking for my husband, they hadn't been able to communicate to each other because of the gaps in service. We were told that different service vessels had even been using hand signals between the boats, because they had no way communicating to each other. This was a side issue to my answered prayer, but it seemed to highlight another need that was addressed and since that event, more mobile phone towers have been erected so that transmission from Hinchinbrook Island and in the channel has improved.

Living by Faith

The Townsville Bulletin Front Page, January 1999

Another example of God answering prayers has been in the provision of work at different times. I've needed to find contracts for work from the welfare industry. This has happened on numerous occasions in the last few years, since I've opened my own business as a social worker. I have needed contract work with different non-government organisations. When I have prayed for more work, amazingly someone had contacted me and just asked, "Would you be available to do some assessments?" Or they have enquired, "Would you be available to provide this training?" This has always come through at just the right time. God has prepared the path for us already.

### Lives saved in boating mishap

God is waiting for us to ask Him and for his provision to be actioned.

Another example of answered prayer is when I've asked for wisdom in how to speak with people in a number of situations. In my role as a social worker, I have been asked to mediate between people who were not getting on well at all. At those times I have asked God for wisdom in how to raise issues with the people involved, how to address topics of concern and I have been amazed at the words of wisdom that God has given me in each of those situations. God has answered my prayer for wisdom.

Praying for people I come across in different situations is an opportunity sometimes I miss, and then I realise afterwards that I could have offered to pray for that person. God brings different people and needs across our path each and every day. Are you thinking of opportunities to pray for people? I can't live without prayer. If we can live with our hearts open and expectant of opportunities to pray for others and to help connect people to God, I know there will be many more prayers answered. Praying gives the opportunity for God to intervene and make a difference in our lives and in other people's lives. If we hesitate and don't offer to pray for someone, we miss out on the blessing of answered prayer and of being an encouragement.

## What ifs?

What if I don't have time to pray? Make time!

What if I am too busy? When we are busy and the schedule is hectic, that is especially when I need to pray. When we are frantic, when under pressure, I need God's wisdom and guidance even more. You may have heard of the saying that you're "too busy not to pray."

What if I don't know how to pray? So how do we pray? We can start by saying "hi God". When we wake up in the morning, it's a brand new day. Start with, "Thank you, God, for today. This is what is on my mind this morning. This is what I'm looking at today. Can you help me with this? How can I be a blessing to others? Help me to encourage others today." It's the time to have a conversation with God and get to know him, which means we need to have time where we're listening for God. That means that we are not doing all the talking.

## Three actions you can take as a result of reading this chapter

1. Consider the question: What is holding you back from talking with God?

2. What is the worst thing that can happen if I pray more?

3. What is a way I could make a habit of praying more daily?

### Additional information and resources

"Is anyone among you in trouble? Let them pray. Is anyone happy? Let them sing songs of praise" (James 5:13, New International Version).

How to pray – A study using The Lord's Prayer as a template. See website http://www.amandanickson.com.au/

More information on prayer can be found on the website: http://www.amandanickson.com.au/ including resources on a seven-day challenge and a 30-day challenge to prayer.

*Chapter 4*

# Busy bees fly
## Use your talents

Do you think you could tap dance to that song? Yes, really! Before I get to songs and dances, let us consider our talents and how to go about using them.

Why do we need to think about our talents? By using them, we can bless others, not to mention provide us with a great deal of satisfaction, because our talents tend to be skills or abilities through which we excel. They give us an opportunity to shine. Whether using your talent serves and blesses one person or a whole community, it is there to be used and enjoyed by yourself and others. It has been given to you to be used.

I found this directing a musical, which brought together a whole community. You can also get satisfaction from baking a cake or a meal for a family or individual in need. Friendships and connections are formed and built on in these situations. When we use our talents, you might have heard of the saying "if you don't use it, you lose it."

"You are the light of the world. A town built on a hill cannot be hidden. Neither do people light a lamp and put it under a bowl. Instead, they put it on a stand, and it gives light to everyone in the house in the same way. Let your light shine before others, that they may see your good deeds and glorify your father in heaven" (Matthew 15:14-16, New International Version).

The Bible also talks about the parable of the talents in Matthew 25:14-21 and in 1 Corinthians 12:14-27. This parable talks about being faithful with the talents you have been given and multiplying them or taking steps to make them grow and develop. The Bible talks about the different parts of the body and how each part is equally important and not all of us are the ears or the eyes. But we each have a role to play to make up the body as a whole.

What is a talent? A natural ability or skill that is God-given.

How can we use our talents? I am going to give some examples from my life of how I have used mine. I come from a musical background and love being involved in directing and producing musical events. In the early nineties, I was thinking about doing a musical, but that would require several steps of faith. I was living in the small mining town of Middlemount in Central Queensland. At that time, I was a pastor's wife and a music director and decided I'd like to do a children's musical called the Bee-Attitudes, by Jimmy and Carol Owens.

At the time we had a church of less than 20 people and this musical had over 30 people in the cast. Where was I going to find these people to be the main characters in a musical? The musical captures the hearts and imaginations of children of all ages. Through his "imaginifying glass", Sylvester Sylvester transported us to the charming world of Queen Bea and her kingdom. Lots of valuable lessons and adventures ensue that teach us about love and responsibilities to one another and to God. The colourful cast included such delightful characters as Honey Bee, Harmony, Wilmer, Can Bee, Praise Bee, Glory Bee and all the Bee-lievers. And then there was Mr Bertrand Bumble who literally stumbled into the story.

So just starting to do a major activity as a small church in a little mining town of approximately 3,000 people took many steps of faith. I had never produced a children's music before, and I wasn't sure I could do it. However, God was in it and supplied the right people to fill all the parts. In the end, the cast involved almost the whole of Middlemount Assembly of God church, and many others from the town's other churches including the Logos church and from the Anglican church. Some children in the cast were not members of any church.

Since I was a child, I had been encouraged to listen to classical music and I started learning piano when I was 10 years old. I loved it and would practice piano every school morning, before breakfast. I had the opportunity to attend a school where there were choirs and an orchestra and chamber music groups, and musical productions. I did the three unit music subject as one of my subjects for my Higher School Certificate. I was a school house music captain and had the opportunity to teach and conduct a choir. I loved music. I had musical skills, and some would say talent, which I loved to use. Fast forward a few years since my final school days and I find myself in a small mining town in central Queensland in a tiny church. And I decided I would like to direct a musical as a community event involving most of the church and children as key cast members.

There were not even enough singers or people in the church to cover the cast. What was I thinking? I felt led by God to do it. And a few women in the church were very supportive and caught the vision for it and what they could do in terms of bringing the community together. Singers from other churches were approached and friends of friends. And we ended up with almost enough people, a couple of key characters were missing. And I remember thinking to ask a particular family, not involved in any of the churches in town, if their son would like to play a key role. Which he did. And he did a super job!

One of my friends in the church was a schoolteacher, and also a good tap dancer. When we were in the early stages of planning the musical, she amazingly offered to do a tap dance in one of the songs. I said, "Do you think you could do a tap dance in that song?" "Yes," she said. "Really?" I questioned. I was just amazed at God, giving her an opportunity to use and showcase her talent in this particular musical!

Teaching the songs and learning the parts was relatively easy for me. It was all the other organising that goes into a musical production that took a lot more effort. For example, who could design and sew costumes. How could I get a backdrop? I had minimal sewing skills. God provided a wonderful, generous and gracious volunteer, a woman in our church, who designed and sewed all the costumes. We had a working bee to paint the backdrop on my driveway one Saturday afternoon. Having confidence in people's ability to do a part helped give them competence, but not all of the cast were present even for one of the several rehearsals, including the final dress rehearsals before the performances. In the way that these things usually work, it seemed impossible for the musical to come together. I'm so glad my God is the one who makes the impossible become possible.

## Busy bees fly

As the performance for the town of Middlemount came closer, I was getting excited in my spirit about what God was going to do. I just knew there would be a full house, and this would have an impact on the town. The local football club was packed with about 140 people seated as well as stage crew and a cast of 30, including 14 children from four years of age upwards. There was a tangible feeling of the presence of God as the as the performance began. Some people in the audience began to cry as soon as the first song began, overwhelmed by the presence of God. The musical went brilliantly, and the children were fantastic. One of the main characters was a five-year old boy who did his part superbly.

Many other little miracles never ceased to amaze me. For example, God's provision of suitable sound equipment and the personnel with the skill and talent to operate it. The list was endless. We got some very positive feedback. The High school invited us to do another performance of the Bee-Attitudes as part of its cultural festival. This was yet another miracle. We received so much positive feedback - all to God's glory. I believe it was a great witness to the town.

**The Bee- Attitudes, singers**

A couple of years later, my husband and I had moved to Townsville and were in a new church and I was part of the music team. I was again thinking of the opportunity to direct a musical. This time I looked at the musical called *The Witness*, which is a version of the story of Jesus, His death on the cross and the resurrection. Again, there were doubts and challenges in filling key positions, but this was a much larger church. We were able to fill all the main parts and had some singers for the choir or chorus from members of the church. It came together and we got a very good review in the local newspaper, The Townsville Bulletin.

Another way I found to use my talents with my social work training, has been to present conference papers at social work conferences. This immediately put me outside my comfort zone, having to do public speaking in front of a group of peers who probably knew more than me in whatever area I was speaking on. Yet, it was an opportunity to share knowledge and practice wisdom from my work in the field. I took on the challenge. Each time I have presented a conference paper, whether at national conferences, state conferences or at international conferences, I have been well received.

When you begin to take steps of faith, you "put yourself out there", you put yourself on the line. If you have an area of expertise, you could be sharing it. Take a step of faith to use your talents.

## What ifs

You might be at a point where you are considering a step of faith, but then doubts come in. You start to have second thoughts about it. Your mind might say to you, "I'm not sure I can do this." Let me remind you, that when we are weak, He is strong. When we acknowledge our weakness, as I have done over and over, God has provided.

Another doubt or negative thought could be, "I don't have everything I need to do this." That's okay. That has certainly been my experience. At each step along the way, God has miraculously provided for whatever the next step or need is.

If you have a talent that you have been keeping hidden, or you haven't been sure about using it, I encourage you to use it.

## Three actions you can take as a result of reading this chapter

1. Take a step of faith to do that thing you've been thinking or dreaming about.

2. Dream big. What if you *do* act on your idea? What is the first step you can take?

3. Talk with a trusted friend about your idea and plan the next steps

### Additional information and resources

Information on different careers, in case you need some ideas on the next steps to get there!
https://www.thebalancecareers.com/free-career-aptitude-tests-2059813

## Chapter 5

# Throw me a lifeline
## Trusting God

"Never have children", my Mum had once said to me. How I ended up not following her advice and trusting God instead will become clear in this chapter.

Trusting God involves a step or steps of faith. At times that step might seem like a small step. At times it can seem like leaping over a chasm. So why would I trust God? Trust, in a similar way to faith, throws me a lifeline direct from God. It connects me to Him in a greater way. The Bible commands us to trust God. And I believe in the Word of God and the importance of being obedient to it, even when that is hard and seems impossible.

God is faithful and true and keeps His word to us. The book of Lamentations 3:22-23 says: "Because of the Lord's great love, we are not consumed for His compassions never fail. They are new every morning. Great is your faithfulness" (New International Version).

So why trust God?

1. If we trust Him with big things, we receive big rewards.
2. If we trust God, we have a greater opportunity for fulfillment.
3. There is great satisfaction in seeing God at work.
4. To trust someone is to allow vulnerability and to give over control, and that takes faith.
5. There is a risk, but rewards are great.
6. In fact, taking a step of faith is a way to conquer fear and overcome fear.

It is important that we trust in God. "The fear of human opinion disables trusting in God who protects you" (Proverbs 29:25, The Message Translation). Another translation of the same verse is that, "The fear of man brings a snare, but whoever trusts you and puts his confidence in the Lord will be exalted and safe" (Amplified Bible). The alternative to trusting God is trusting men. Mankind is fallible and imperfect. I have come to the conclusion that it is much better to put my trust in God.

What do I mean by trust? Trust is to have a firm belief and confidence in the truth, reliability and ability of someone or something.

A couple of examples in my life come to mind. Starting with a big issue – whether I would choose to have children or not! In my family background, mental illness and mental health issues have been a very big factor. My sister has lived with chronic schizophrenia, a significant mental illness, ever since the age of about 15. She lives a good life now, but there have been periods where she has been quite debilitated, with numerous hospital admissions when life became difficult to cope with, or medications had to be reviewed or changed. To me, it was one of the saddest things to see – a young woman full of potential as a promising musician who seemed to have her future taken away by this illness.

My father had had a period in hospital for his "nerves" – I assume some kind of nervous breakdown, when I was in high school. It was not talked about openly. There was a lot of stigma attached to such illness.

When my mother was about to have surgery one day for a heart condition, about to get a pacemaker, she said to me, "Amanda, never have children". I assumed she chose this moment to share her thoughts on this subject as it was very important to her and she was worried about her surgery and whether it would be successful - whether she would survive and be able to have this conversation with me at a later date. I knew this came from her concern about mental illness, the worry it could cause, and her belief that it was largely a genetic disorder. The whole debate about mental illness being hereditary vs being caused or triggered by environment was something I was aware of.

Being an adult but also someone who was very close to my mother, I thought then that this must be the right decision for me. I respected her, trusted her and loved her - totally. I had taken this advice to heart. Imagine a few years later when I met my future husband, Daryl, and as we were having conversations about a joint future together, I said, "I never want to have children." Daryl was very trusting and accepted that that was where my thinking on the matter was at that time. He said that he just believed that I would change my mind over time. I had said to him very clearly, "I don't think so", but Daryl assured me he was happy to accept me on those terms. I continued to be a career woman early in our marriage and had no interest at all in having children, but I knew that my husband wanted children. This was not a tension point between us at all, but it was a wrestling point between me and God as I was trying to work out what was God's will for me in this situation.

I can remember once being in a church service at Emerald where a visiting pastor had a word of encouragement for someone who was afraid of having children. I thought the word was for me, but then he went on and talked about someone who feared childbirth. It was not childbirth that I was afraid of, but rather of mental illness being genetically passed down to my children. Looking back on this time now, it was as if I thought that genetics was more powerful than God. In fact, God is bigger than science and genetics – He created it all! I spent a lot of time praying and seeking God. And it dawned on me that deciding to have a child was like a step of faith. Would I trust God enough that he would take care of the health and wellbeing of my child or my children? Would I take that step of faith?

After five years of marriage, I trusted God enough to take a step of faith and have our first child. Our beautiful daughter, Jessica was born. After another three years, we had another daughter, Danielle. And then after another three years, our son Timothy. I have been blessed with these three, beautiful children. Children are such a blessing from God. That decision to not follow my mother's advice and words, as someone who wants to honour her parents, was hard. But I chose to follow a higher authority, to act on the Word of God, which says to trust God in all I do. That was a hard decision and difficult step of faith for me. But God has not let me down. Children bring so much joy.

I found that Proverbs helped me at this time, with verses saying: "Trust in and rely confidently on the Lord with all your heart and do not rely on your own insight or understanding. In all your ways, know and acknowledge and recognise him. And he will make your paths straight and smooth removing obstacles that block your way" (Proverbs 3:5-6, Amplified version).

Another example of having to trust God with my children is when as young adults, one of my children in particular had some major struggles with mental health. This was an extremely difficult time for her, but also for me. I felt guilty. I felt alone. I would be thinking - has she inherited mental illness because of my family? In fact, there are significant mental health issues on both sides of our family. Daryl's mother and brother had significant mental health issues as well. My sister had had significant mental health issues. And now I was facing a time with my daughter having very significant mental health issues.

I had to employ so much faith and prayer and trust with this situation. One of the difficulties with someone experiencing mental health issues is that in Australian society, there is still so much stigma attached to mental health that it is difficult even to seek the normal support you would through friends. Usually if I had a family member with an illness, I would be seeking support in my church, asking for prayer and asking for prayer with other Christians I know. However, out of respect for my daughter's wishes not to share information about her situation, and to respect her privacy, I did not do this. My husband and I prayed and prayed. Thankfully, she is now doing really, really well. I believe through this experience of illness my daughter has come to know Jesus her personal saviour in a deeper way. And she is now back in church, serving God and looking to a bright future. And if you were wondering, I have her permission to share what I have written about this in this chapter.

I found this period in my life very trying. It was one of those situations where I was saying, "But God! I trusted you to have children and now, this very thing that I feared has happened!" But God was still in control. I'm reminded that, "And we know that in all things, God works for the good of those who love him, who have been called according to his purpose" (Romans 8:28, New International Version) In the season that we went through, whilst the Devil might have had evil intent and plans for my daughter, God had a bigger plan and she will now have an amazing testimony that can encourage and inspire others who might struggle with mental health issues.

Another example in my life of having to trust God is the decision to get married. There isn't a decision much bigger than that. It's an exercise in trust, trusting another person to share your life with and making a declaration before God and those people present that I will do this "until death do us part". I know God honours our decisions. And at times I laugh, inwardly, wondering how is it that God can put such opposites together! I have surmised that it is so that we can complement each other – where one is weak, the other is strong. When I met Daryl and got to know him, it was his love for Christ and his passion to share Jesus with others that I was really attracted to. We are opposites in so many ways. He's the extrovert, I'm the introvert. He is loud, I am quiet. He likes to do things spontaneously, whereas I like to plan and organise well in advance. The decision to marry and share one's life with someone else is a test of trust because we're trusting our life with another person and joining everything to become one. This is a major exercise in trust and yet the blessings are great. It is a step of faith!

I have now been married over 35 years and certainly we have had our challenges and ups and downs, but it's wonderful because I live with someone who supports me and loves me, no matter what.

Another example of trust in my life is something as simple as going to see a doctor and trusting their expertise and knowledge to deal with the situation in my life. There have been times when I have been very stressed and anxious, and I have needed to be on anxiety medication for a number of years. A trusted doctor is the person who first prescribed medication for me. And I was horrified at one level. But then at another, I thought, if I had any other medical condition that could be rectified or treated with a tablet such as high blood pressure, a heart condition, anything else, I wouldn't hesitate, but because this was to do with my mental health, I was doubting.

So, as a step of faith, I have been on this medication and it made a huge difference to my ability to function on a daily basis. My doctor also recommended at one point that I should see a psychologist or social worker and maybe this professional could help with my anxieties. At this point, part of my mind is saying, "Do I really need this? Haven't I trusted God enough?" But then I thought I would give it a try. And so, I have seen a psychologist a few times at different points in my life when I was particularly stressed and feeling that I was not coping very well. And she was able to give me some great strategies for dealing with my fears and anxiety at that time.

I am sharing this and being vulnerable with you, my readers, because I think, well, God has created these types of specialists and professionals and why not access them? And maybe someone reading this needs to be assured that it is okay and in fact very sensible and practical to see a professional counsellor, psychologist or social worker when we go through difficulties in life. I hope this encourages someone that we don't have to go through struggles alone, even when we are trusting God. If it is going to help me to function and operate as a wife, a mother, a worker, a friend, as a part of a church, then I highly recommend seeing professionals for help. If you do have mental health issues or a mental illness, seeking professional help and opening up to this "stranger", even when assured of confidentiality, is a big step of faith. I assure you for me it was so worthwhile and the help and support, and the rewards, were great.

## What if's

What about genetics? God is bigger than biology, and He is able.

What if my children end up getting sick? God is still in control and He is able to heal and restore. This happened to me and I know God is still in control. He is able, and even through the situation of my daughter having a difficult time with mental illness, my daughter has come to a closer relationship with God.

What if it comes out that I have mental health issues?

Well, I'll hope that by my disclosing my own struggles with anxiety, that it will help overcome the stigma of mental health and mental illness. We need to talk about it. One in five people in Australia have a mental health issue. The statistics are higher for depression.

1 John 3:23 says: "So these are his commands that we continually place our trust in the name of his son, Jesus Christ. And that we keep loving one another, just as he commanded us" (The Passion Translation.)

And in Romans 15:13: "May the God of hope fill you with all joy and peace as you trust in him so that you may overflow with hope by the power of the Holy Spirit" (New International Version)

## Three actions you can take as a result of reading this chapter

1. What is holding you back from a decision to trust?

2. What is the worst thing that can happen if you do trust?

3. When have you trusted before and seen great outcomes?

**Additional information and resources**

https://www.beyondblue.org.au/

To find a social worker or psychologist, you can look on their professional association websites, see links:

https://www.aasw.asn.au/find-a-social-worker/search/

https://www.psychology.org.au/Find-a-Psychologist

*Chapter 6*

# Hang out with encouragers
## Encouragement

For months I had been thinking I can't do it, it's too hard for me. "You can do it", my friends encouraged. What could make me think differently? Well, I have found that encouragement is the most amazing thing. Why? Because encouragement makes a difference. It is powerful! I will come to the rest of my story shortly.

**Why hang out with encouragers?**

Encouragement makes a difference. It can move our thinking from "it's impossible" to "maybe I can do this, maybe it's possible."

Optimists lift your spirits and things seem more possible. Whereas negativity kills creativity. Being believed in by someone is really powerful and believing in someone else is powerful. Turning self-talk from negative self-talk to positive self-talk makes a huge difference. Researchers estimate that we think about 50,000 to 70,000 thoughts a day, and that about 80% of those thoughts are negative (https://www.jackcanfield.com/blog/negative-self-talk/).

It has also been found that negative thoughts can make us physically sick.

In contrast, the Bible teaches us the importance of our thinking: "Finally, brothers and sisters, whatever is true, whatever is noble, whatever is right, whatever is pure, whatever is lovely, whatever is admirable. If anything is excellent or praiseworthy, think about such things" (Philippians 4:8, New International Version). Similarly, "Do not conform to the pattern of this world, but be transformed by the renewing of your mind. Then you will be able to test and approve what God's will is - his good pleasing and perfect will" (Romans 12:2, New International Version).

So, what does encouragement mean? It can be defined as a means "to give support, confidence or hope to someone. To cheer, to champion, to hearten, inspire, uplift, and motivate."

What is self-talk? Self-talk is your internal dialogue. It is influenced by your subconscious mind and it reveals your thoughts, beliefs, questions, and ideas. Self-talk can be both negative and positive. It can be encouraging, or it can be distressing. Often connected to self-talk, when it is negative, is self-doubt, a lack of faith in oneself, a feeling of doubt or uncertainty about one's abilities and actions.

An example in my own life of the power of encouragement is how I managed to complete a PhD in social work. As a young child in primary school, I had dyslexia. In spelling tests, I would only get 2 out of 20 words correct. Week after week, I would study and learn my words, but no matter what I did, I got them wrong. Fortunately, I had parents who noticed I was struggling with my learning and put in a lot of extra work to help me learn, to read and write. They tutored me every night. My mother became involved with SPELD NSW, a non- government organisation that supported families with children with specific learning difficulties and raised awareness about this. My Mum became a spokesperson and Vice President of SPELD. I hated reading and avoided it as much as possible. It was the worst and hardest activity for me. By the time I finished primary school, I was able to read, yet I was still not the best at spelling. I overcame dyslexia and managed to get to university and do my Bachelor of Social Work. When I finished that degree, I thought I would never go back to a university and study again and do more reading and writing.

Some 13 years later, I found myself interested in doing a Master of Social Work at James Cook University. I was amazed when I received my first ever distinction grade for a social work assignment. I finished my Master's degree in 1999. Six years later in 2005, I decided I would really like to do some research into peer group supervision of social workers in rural and remote Australia. I applied to do a PhD, not even knowing if I would be accepted because I hadn't done Honours or the usual pre-requisites, but I had done some research projects in the workplace and had presented at some conferences. I was accepted to do a PhD and encouraged by my supervisors who considered the topic very worthwhile. That encouragement made a great difference starting my studies.

However, as many people know who have done any research or a higher degree, it can be a bit like doing an endurance race, not a sprint. Soon I was juggling a full-time job, a part-time PhD, a family and church commitments. For a long time, the PhD would come last in my priorities. Then, when I put in the time and effort and progressed with the research, I would get discouraged. I had supportive supervisors, however, when I got feedback on my written chapters that needed a lot of work or to be re-done, I was discouraged. I knew it wouldn't be easy, but this was so much harder than I had anticipated. Self-doubt started creeping in.

I had already experienced mild depression and anxiety related to the heavy workload and general stress. It thrives in environments where you are trying to study and doubting yourself. My anxiety increased significantly, and this was quite crippling for me during this time. (See more information on anxiety at the end of this chapter.)

A handful of my very close friends and immediate family were encouragers – my cheer squad who helped get me over the line! A couple of friends from church would pray and believe with me that I could do it. I wasn't so sure, but because they believed in me, they helped me think it may be possible for me to finish my PhD. I got to a point where I thought, I have got to finish this – I had put in so many hours and so much effort – I couldn't not finish, as otherwise all those hours and sacrifices would have been for nothing. Some friends would encourage by phone, by email, with coffees, with hugs – willing me on, encouraging me and they kept believing in me. I had to keep saying to myself, my favourite verse: "I can do all things through Christ who strengthens me" (Philippians 4:13, New International Version). I would go forward, but then I would doubt it. I felt like a yo-yo, constantly up and down. Some of my close colleagues at my workplace at the university were also very encouraging. That was like gold. That encouraged me.

I even found a way to encourage myself! Instead of continually thinking about how much I still had to go with the PhD, the mountain always ahead of me, I started keeping a journal of what

## Hang out with encouragers

I had done each day. The entries could say "wrote 200 words on *x*, edited *x*, contacted *x*." Over the course of a week, I could see the progress I was making, little by little. This encouraged me that it was happening and moving forward. It was still a struggle, but I could see that I was making progress.

God really strengthened me to do this seemingly insurmountable mountain of an assignment called a PhD. I have heard some people refer to this as a "Pretty Hard Document", and I agree. When I finally submitted my thesis in 2015, that was such a huge relief. However, imagine my feelings when six months later, one of the two examiners of the thesis wanted me to rewrite three or four chapters because she did not think it was of a high enough standard. I was devastated! And exhausted by this time.

I could have easily given up at that point. But thankfully, I had a couple of close friends who said, again, "You can do it". They just kept encouraging me over and over, which helped tremendously to get me to that finish line. I finished my PhD and passed!

Another challenging situation I found myself in was my lack of fitness and my desire to walk the Camino Way, a pilgrimage walk across Spain. This is a very long walk, and I knew I needed to work on my fitness. Once again, I had a close friend who encouraged me and said, "You will be able to do it. Just keep taking small steps, and gradually, do more and more walking." With that encouragement and starting with walking small distances, my friend Louise and I were able to build our fitness over several months. There is always a way to get to a goal, especially when you hang out with encouragers.

I find that I am constantly needing to challenge and change my self-talk. I started thinking "maybe I can do it" rather than "I can't do it". Changing my thinking, noticing my inner self-talk, and consciously replacing negative thoughts with positive ones made a big difference to my mindset.

Amanda at her PhD Graduation, 2017

## What ifs

1. You might say, "I don't know any encouraging people or positive people". Well, it's time to find some. You could try going to a local church.

2. All my friends discourage me or are negative or critical. Well, it's time to find some new friends.

3. I am not sure I can change my thinking. Well, practice makes perfect. Keep practising some deliberate positive self-talk every day.

## Three actions you can take as a result of reading this chapter

1. Find some positive, encouraging people to hang out with and move away from those negative people in your life.

2. Think of the blessings and good things in your life and give thanks for them.

3. Ignore any negative things that have been spoken over you. Reflect on what the Bible says about you (see the resource section at the end of this chapter) and practice replacing negative self-talk with positive self-talk.

## Additional information and resources

What does the Bible say about me and about encouragement? It tells us to remember that "I am fearfully and wonderfully made" (Psalm 139:13-15, New International Version). God has created me for a purpose. With this in mind, we should "encourage one another and build each other up" (1 Thessalonians 5:11, New International Version). 2 Corinthians 13:11, 1 Thessalonians 4:18 and Hebrews 3:13 also talk about encouraging one another.

For more information on specific learning difficulties, including dyslexia, information is available at this website: https://www.speldnsw.org.au/

Anxiety:

Further information on anxiety can be found on the beyond blue website, see the link below.

Anxiety is more than just feeling stressed or worried. While stress and anxious feelings are a common response to a situation where we feel under pressure, they usually pass once the stressful situation has passed, or the stressor is removed. Everyone feels anxious from time to time. When anxious feelings don't go away, happen without any particular reason or make it hard to cope with daily life it may be a sign of an anxiety condition.

Anxiety is the most common mental health condition in Australia. On average, one in four people, one in three women and one in five men will experience anxiety at some stage in their life. In a 12-month period, over 2 million Australians experience anxiety. (https://www/beyondblue.org.au/the-facts/anxiety)

That's a lot of people! We all need that encouragement.

*Chapter 7*

# A mother's heart
## Share your burdens

Having concerns for the wellbeing of one's children is natural. However, unhealthy worry is not helpful for anyone. Sharing my worries gave me relief, even though the situation was still there.

So why is it that sharing burdens is a good thing? Firstly, sharing your burdens reduces the load. There is a saying that "a burden shared is a burden halved". I believe that to be true. Secondly, it's scriptural to share your burdens: "Share each other's burdens, and in this way, obey the law of Christ" (Galatians 6:2, New Living Translation). Another translation says: "Carry each other's burdens, and in this way, you will fulfill the law of Christ" (New International Version) Thirdly, it is when we share our burdens that solutions become possible.

An important part of sharing a burden with a Christian friend is that we can pray together. In that way, we can "move the mountain"

– shifting the burden, rather than simply talking about how heavy it is. I have found the power of prayer when two or three (believers) are gathered together is amazing. We are not alone facing struggles and carrying that burden by ourselves.

Sometimes, the burdens we carry include emotional baggage from the past, weighing us down with unresolved issues. Being set free from the weight of the past can be liberating, transformative and gives us a new lease on life.

What is a burden? A burden is a load, usually a heavy load at that. To burden is to cause worry, hardship or distress. Worry is when we feel or to cause to feel anxious or troubled about actual or potential problems. It is to fret, to brood, agonise, to distress or to trouble. Another definition is emotional baggage, which is the feelings you have about your past and the things that have happened to you, which often have a negative effect on your behaviour and attitudes.

An example from my own life about sharing a burden occurred a few years ago when my son was really struggling in Grade 12, his final year of high school. Tim did not like school at all. He was not academic, so he had especially been enrolled in this particular high school because it had a sporting program that he could be a part of that counted sport as one or two of his subjects. Sports were Tim's strength and passion. At the end of Grade 10, the school announced that the sports program he was part of would not be continuing for the following two years, when Tim was to be in Grades 11 and 12. You can imagine how he felt about this! There were many days that Tim would not go to school and I was forever phoning the school, giving an apology and making some excuse that he was unwell. Because to me it was so important to get that Year 12 certificate completed. I talked with Tim about options such as leaving school and starting work or a trade, however, Tim knew it was important to get a Year 12 certificate, to do anything in the future. He hung in there – just!

At this time, I was meeting weekly with a close Christian friend of mine from church, Bronnie. When we spent time together, I was able to share with her my worries and concerns about my son and how could I get him to school. We would pray together, pray for a breakthrough, pray for ideas, pray for wisdom. And somehow, Tim got through Year 12. It is actually quite miraculous that he was able to get his Year 12 certificate because he was out of school for so many days. I don't know how the school managed it, but they did.

Being able to speak with another mother who had also had struggles with some of her children gave me reassurance that we would get there in the end. Bronnie and I would pray for her children and my children, our family situations, our work needs and knew that we had given every situation safely into God's hands. We knew and believed that God would provide a way where there seems to be no way. Bronnie and I believed God could make the impossible become possible.

My son finished Year 12 and I thought I'd finished the hardest task parents have - getting their children through school and safely into adulthood. I was wrong. After school finished, there was the lengthy period of time where Tim was unemployed - unable to find work and find direction. Again, I shared my burden. This time I shared my burden with another close Christian friend, Louise, and we would pray together seeking God's wisdom and intervention in this situation. A mother's heart cannot help but worry about their children's welfare. I could see the effect of being unemployed was having on Tim – he was losing hope for the future. Being able to share my struggles with Louise meant that I was not getting more and more stressed, but able to stay in faith, believing for an answer

– believing that God would come through and have an answer for Tim.

Finally, at this time, Tim went to a new church and found his passion for God. He began to attend Bible College. He was offered a job in a café next to the gym he attended. It was perfect – making healthy shakes and coffees was right up Tim's alley. Later, he was offered work in the church in their cafe, making coffees and catering there. I was so excited! Not only did Tim have a job, but the fact that Tim had restored his relationship with God and was going forward strongly in his faith filled my heart with so much joy! When God answers prayers, sometimes it is over and above what we could possibly have thought or imagined.

Another example of sharing my burden is when my daughter had some struggles with mental health and then was really unwell for a period of time. During this period, I was able to share my anguish, my guilt, my worries with my girlfriend, Louise, and pray and believe together that God was in the situation and had my daughter in his hands. Just being able to talk and cry with another person who supported me emotionally, but also directed me to prayer, made a fantastic difference. My daughter still had mental health issues at that time, but I was confident that God was in the situation and that it would work out.

Another example is at different times, I would be struggling to focus on my own work and get it done. Whether that means needing to get some writing done, whether that was getting marking done for my role at the university. Again, I would meet with my friend Louise and just share my burdens and my inability to focus. And we would pray together believing for God to give me wisdom and for God to help me to focus. And God answered these prayers. Being able to pray together with a woman of faith really made a difference, because when two or three people are gathered together, Christ is with us.

## What ifs?

Maybe you are thinking, "How can I share my concerns with someone else? It's personal." Yes, it is personal. But if you can find someone you can trust, who will keep matters confidential, that can make all the difference. I have found if I'm open and allow myself to be vulnerable with someone else that deepens the relationship and friendship. And often that trust will be reciprocated with them sharing something that's burdening them as well.

Another concern might be that you feel you can't talk about it because you might cry or make a fool of yourself. I can tell you, it's much better if you do share it. Being emotional is part of the human condition. It's the way God has created us. If you are able to share with a friend who was supportive, if you cry or are emotional, I am sure that it will be okay.

Another concern might be people seeing that I don't have it all together. Well, the truth is none of us do. We don't have it altogether all of the time. We all have times where we're struggling with concerns and worries, and I guarantee you, if you're able to share your burden with someone you trust and be able to pray together, the relief of that burden shared and of answered prayers is amazing.

## Three actions you can take as a result of reading this chapter

1. Be brave and share your burdens with a close and trusted friend and pray together

2. Pray that God will act or change the circumstances, the burden, expectantly. Pray using scripture from the Word of God.

3. Be prepared to reciprocate. This means to be available to hear and support your friends share their burdens too. That is what friendship is about. Good friends will listen and not judge.

### Additional information and resources

Psalm 68:19 says, "Praise be to the Lord, to God our Saviour, who daily bears our burdens" (New International Version).

### Emotional baggage

There is a lot more information on emotional baggage that may be helpful. Sometimes it is important to seek professional counselling or help. If you've had a particularly traumatic or abused background, whilst it may be helpful to share some of those burdens with a close friend and pray together, don't underestimate the support and difference seeing a professional can make. See a Social Worker or Psychologist and deal with

## A mother's heart

these issues in the past so that you can move forward in life free of these burdens.

To find a social worker or psychologist, you can look on their professional association websites, see links:

https://www.aasw.asn.au/find-a-social-worker/search/

https://www.psychology.org.au/Find-a-Psychologist

More information is available at https://www.beyondblue.org.au

## Chapter 8

# Creating your own Camino

## Self-compassion and looking after yourself

We all need times of refreshing and replenishing. Like many things in life, we need to plan it and make it a priority, or it doesn't happen. Why do we think we can go on forever, without time off to rest and restore? Jesus himself withdrew from the crowds to spend time alone with God in prayer. In Luke 6:12, "One of those days Jesus went out to a mountainside to pray, and spent the night praying to God" (New International Version). If He needed to spend time alone with God to pray, refresh and replenish, how much more would you and I need to?!

Why do we need to show ourselves self-compassion and look after ourselves?

Firstly, building resilience and reserves is vital. If we give out all the time, our tanks can become empty so that there is nothing left to give. The Bible talks about being refreshed, and that each of us should "repent then and turn to God so that our sins may be wiped out. That times of refreshing may come from the Lord" (Acts 3:19, New International Version). God tells us "I will refresh the weary and satisfy the faint" (Jeremiah 31:25, New International Version).

Secondly, we all need to replenish our tanks as we are not superhuman.

Thirdly, self-care is critical to our ongoing well-being. Knowing what replenishes you is important to find out, because for each person it will be different.

Fourthly, the alternative is exhaustion and burnout, and then we are no use to anyone. Not to our families, our workplaces or our friends and social groups.

An interesting fact is that the World Health Organisation has now classified burnout in its list of conditions. It defines it as "a syndrome conceptualised as resulting from chronic workplace stress that has not been successfully managed". It's really important that we be on the lookout for how we are traveling, both in work and in life in general.

You have probably heard the old proverb by James Howell that "all work and no play, makes Jack a dull boy".

It is important that we look after our own wellbeing because no one else can do it for us.

What is "wellbeing"? It can be defined as a state of being comfortable, healthy and happy, secure and safe.

"To restore" is defined as "to bring back, re-establish, to repair or renovate, give back and rebuild." And "to refresh" is "to give new strength or energy, to reinvigorate, to revitalise, revive or fortify".

"Self-care" is the "ability to refill and refuel oneself in healthy ways" (Gentry (2002) in Cox and Steiner (2013) p.31).

## Walking the Camino

One of the most amazing and refreshing, replenishing times in my life was when, in 2018, I was able to walk the Camino de Santiago, or the Way of Saint James, also referred to as "The Way" or "The Camino" in Spain. It is a pilgrimage to the Spanish city of Santiago de Compostela that many people come to walk from all over the world, some starting in France or from various starting points in Spain. Walking the Camino is a chance to intentionally slow down and move at a human pace, to join a history that is much bigger than any of us individually.

I had wanted to do the Camino walk for a number of years, but never thought that I would be able to because it was overseas and that seemed like an expensive trip. I couldn't see a way of doing it. How could I get the time off work to do it? Could I afford it? I would also have to be fit enough to walk many kilometres a day. And then I heard that a friend of mine from church was looking at walking the Camino Way. She had already planned to go with someone else, but I thought, well, I'll ask, would she mind if I tagged along too? So, I asked my friend Louise, "Would it be possible for me to join you on this trip? Or have you already organised it?" As it turned out, the friend she was originally going with could not go anymore. And she was needing someone to go with or wanted someone to go with her. Perfect! We started planning this trip together probably a year ahead of when we would actually do it. We had so much fun researching it, planning, saving, paying the deposit for our trip, paying off instalments for the cost. We wanted to pay for as much as possible before we went as we could. We were able to plan to visit a few other countries after walking the Camino to make the most of our time overseas and my dream destinations were becoming a reality before my eyes – Italy, Slovenia, the Czech Republic and Hungary were added to the itinerary.

It was a once-in-a-lifetime overseas trip that I had been dreaming of, but more than that, it was giving me the opportunity to spend time walking in nature, which is one of my favourite things to do, in a beautiful, rural part of Spain. In the cool climate of late autumn, going into the winter months, which are exactly the conditions I like for walking. Walking the Camino from Oviedo to Santiago brought me closer to God. Spending the time talking with Him each day helped me gain a different perspective on many of the things that had been happening in my life that had been causing me worry and grief. Those things in the preceding couple of years that had been troubling, exhausting and wearing me down each day. I was amazed by the beauty of the areas that we were walking through. We walked on laneways behind farms, next to little villages, bush tracks through forests, crossing streams and climbing ridges to see beautiful views. We had day after day of stunning scenery, fresh air, and occasionally another pilgrim.

There was great comradery in the small group we were walking with. I was not the fittest person and had doubted that I would be even able to do this walk at all. As the itinerary was at least 20 odd kilometres a day, Louise and I found a vital piece of information - it turned out we were able to walk a shorter distance each day (10 to 14 kilometres a day) and make up the remaining distance with a taxi ride, which suited me and Louise perfectly. I was the least fit in our group of travellers, and yet God provided a way for

## Creating your own Camino

me to do the Camino – to refresh, relax, and be rejuvenated in a beautiful country and be in His presence for the trip. Walking about 12 kilometres a day for two weeks was a lot more physical activity than I would usually do in a day!

**Another path on the Camino Way**

This experience of being wonderfully refreshed and being replenished came after I had a number of years of high stress and anxiety performing in a high-level job at a university and completing a PhD. Anxiety and self-doubt convinced me that I would never finish and would not pass my PhD. I ended up finishing and passing, however the toll on me had been enormous.

**Creating your own Camino**

We cannot all go and do the Camino walk and travel to Spain every time we need to rest and refresh. So, how do we create our own time of refreshing and restoration? I call this "creating your own Camino" experience. It is important to work out what works for you, what replenishes you, and when you feel closest to God. For me, it is when I am in the beauty of nature, whether that is at a beach, looking at a beautiful ocean or a sunrise or sunset or in a rainforest or a National Park - in places of natural beauty. This is when I am closest to God and it does my soul good seeing natural beauty.

Of course, we can't afford to go on special holidays all the time. But I can certainly make a short trip to the nearest park, or beautiful garden or the nearest beach, or go away on a day off or for a weekend to a place that has beautiful walks such as a nearby National Park. This is what I have found that works for me. Having "mini" refreshing breaks and weekends away and short walks helps me get back in touch with God and to feel refreshed. It is important to find what works for you – we are all unique.

I really value quiet time, some time alone. Some people refresh and are rejuvenated in the company of others. Try some different things and work out what works best for you. Another way of refreshing and replenishing for me is spending more time with God. When I prioritise spending time with God, that is when I can feel refreshing in my spirit, which is also very important to me.

For some people, spending time with God might happen every day and that would not be something extra, but for some of us, making extra time can make the difference between being refreshed or being depleted in spirit and worn out. Psalm 23 says: "The Lord is my shepherd. I shall not want. He lets me lie down in green pastures. He leads me beside the still and quiet waters. He refreshes and restores my soul (life); He leads me in the paths of righteousness for His name's sake" (Amplified Version). I believe it is God's will that we be restored and refreshed and not worn out and exhausted.

## Some objections

Someone has asked me, "Isn't looking after yourself selfish?" My answer to that is a resounding "no!" We need to look after ourselves. We are responsible for our own health and well-being. Do not worry about what other people may think.

One way to think about self-care, as suggested by Cox and Steiner (2013), is to consider it to be like a seatbelt. It is something really important to have in place as a safety measure at all times so that we do not get hurt and damaged. If we wait until we are totally stressed and burnt out to plan some self-care, we have left it too late. We need to have an ongoing plan of things happening to look after ourselves.

Another thing people often say is, "Won't people think I'm rude if I say 'no' to a request to do something?" Too bad if they do! We can say "no" politely to requests for our time. Our time is a precious, limited resource! Sometimes I have to say no to some things, even things that sound like a great idea or project, or interesting things I would like to be a part of, because otherwise, if I say yes to everything I am asked to do, I will be "spread too thin" to do any of my responsibilities properly. We need to look after ourselves and sometimes that means being assertive and saying "no". I am one of those people who finds it very hard to say no to anything. I have learned, however, that at times I need to.

## Three actions you can take as a result of reading this chapter

1. Plan and do three things that refresh your body, mind, and spirit each week

2. Try some new things that you haven't tried before (for self-care).

3. Find a place that is refreshing for you that is nearby or do-able on a day off. For example, if you are replenished sitting in nature, where is a place that you can go to nearby? Find a place or activity that works for you and then go there or do that activity.

## Additional information and resources

More Information on self-care, self-compassion and building resilience can be found at Amanda's website: https://www.amandanickson.com.au


## References

Cox and Steiner (2013) *Self-Care in Social Work, A guide for practitioners, supervisors and administrators*; Washington DC, NASW Press

Smullens, S (2015) *Burnout and Selfcare in Social Work, A guidebook for students and those in mental health and related professions* Washington DC, NASW Press

Chapter 9

# Walking for a cause

## Compassion – helping others

Helping where you can and showing compassion and kindness for others actually gives back to us many times over. I was raised to think of others. At the school I attended, each class would be given a charity to raise funds for during the year. This usually meant holding cake stalls and my mother, my grandmother and I would always bake many cakes for these. They taught me to be generous to people less fortunate than me. This was the norm in the environment I was raised in. It made me appreciate that I had more than enough and could provide a little help to others who may not be as fortunate in life.

**Why is it important to think about others and to have compassion?**

Firstly, doing something for others, does something in you. It makes me realise how fortunate I am compared to someone who, for example, has a medical condition affecting their mobility and speech; or someone whose house has just burnt down or a whole number of other situations. It helps us be thankful for what we have.

Secondly, we have been commanded to show compassion and we need to imitate Jesus's examples of demonstrating compassion to others. The parable of the Good Samaritan is a well-known story in the Bible which talks about a man helping someone who'd been robbed, beaten up and left for dead on the road (Luke 10:25-37, New International Version). He needed medical help, accommodation and food. The Good Samaritan, a stranger to this man, did just that – bound his wounds, transported him to some accommodation, paid for this and some food and stated to the inn keeper (think motel owner) to look after the man and that he would be back to pay for any other expenses to cover the needs of this person. When was the last time you helped someone who was homeless? Or helped someone to access a doctor who had no money or transport? The Good Samaritan did not judge the person – he simply showed kindness and acted with compassion and helped him out. I constantly remind myself when confronted with different needs - what would Jesus do? We are not here to judge, but to follow in Jesus's footsteps and that means He wants us, His people, to show compassion.

Thirdly, it can inspire others. For the last few years, I have been doing a number of fundraising walks for different causes, which is part of a strategy to get myself to walk more, to get fitter. What I have found was that I have been getting feedback from different people about how I had inspired them. Wow! Really? Who would have thought that! Something that I had really been doing for myself, whilst raising funds for different causes, was making a difference for the organisations I was fundraising for, and also encouraging others to think about doing something similar.

## Walking for a cause

Fourthly, you can make a difference. Every time we do something for someone else, that one act of kindness or generosity could save that person's life. You don't know what people are going through. A small act of kindness can be the difference that helps someone who might be at the point of breakdown and turn it into a breakthrough.

Fifthly, whatever you do for others, is what we are doing for Christ himself. The Bible teaches us to "love your neighbour as yourself" (Matthew 22:39, New International Version) and "let us not become weary in doing good" (Galatians 6:9, New International Version). We are also reminded that, "Therefore, as God's chosen people, holy and dearly loved, clothe yourselves with compassion, kindness, humility, gentleness and patience" (Colossians 3:12, New International Version). What the Bible teaches is quite the opposite to what many people in the media say about putting ourselves first. That we should be "number one". I'm not afraid to be different to what is popular in the media. The Bible teaches in Matthew 20:26-28 that: "Anyone wanting to be a leader among you must be your servant. And if you want to be right at the top, you must serve like a slave" (New International Version). "Your attitude must be like my own, for I, the Messiah, did not come to be served, but to serve, and to give my life as a ransom for many." (The Living Bible). For us, to be first, we need to put ourselves last – the opposite of popular culture.

What is compassion? Compassion is a feeling of deep sympathy and sorrow for the misfortune of others plus a strong desire to alleviate that suffering - that is, doing something about it. It is about taking some action.

Compassion requires the capacities for emotional intelligence and empathy entails the discipline of being able to surrender and to be moved by the emotional experiences and needs of others.

Compassion is important to God. He shows his compassion for all men and wants us to follow his example because "the Lord is gracious and righteous; our God is full of compassion" (Psalm 116:5, New International Version).

## Examples in my life

Around the time my parents separated, while I was a teenager, I recall being on the receiving end of compassion on one particular occasion which made a big impact in my life. My mum, sister and I went to live with my maternal grandmother who I affectionately called "Lady". I had told the Youth Leader about it at the church I was attending as I was staying at a different address and had a different phone number, which I gave him, and had let them know so that I could still get a lift to youth group. I had been a little worried about whether my Mum, my sister and I would be judged by the church as my mum had chosen to separate from my father. It had been a situation of worsening domestic violence. The next day, the Youth Leader rang my new phone number and asked to speak to my mum.

I did not know what he was doing! As he had heard from me about the separation, he apparently then asked my mum, "Is there anything we can do to help you? Do you need anything?" That act of care and concern and compassion in a phone call meant so much to my Mum and me. We felt accepted and loved by the church, despite the circumstances we were in.

My decision to become a social worker was linked to my Christian faith and wanting to be able to show compassion as part of my daily work. Social workers can experience the privilege of helping others and can find great joy and satisfaction in doing this. Outside of my working life, there are still many ways I can find to show compassion.

## Walking for a cause

An example of intentionally showing compassion happened a few years ago when I decided to participate in the Cancer Council's Relay for Life, which is a fundraising event. The reason? Two of the pastor's wives in my church had both had been diagnosed with cancer and were undergoing various treatments for the cancers. At that time, I was trying to think, how can I show them that we are thinking of them and supporting them, but also supporting the bigger picture of other people, living with cancer, battling cancer and surviving since cancer. I consulted the Pastor and then organised a team from our church who participated in the Relay for Life and I made sure that the people that were affected by cancer knew what we were doing and why. I actually made it a "prayer walk". Not only were we walking all night (The Relay for Life means the team do laps around an oval from 3:00pm on a Saturday afternoon until 8:00am the following morning, usually using a roster), but we were praying as we walked. And we raised funds from donations by sponsors for the Cancer Council. While I was doing the event, we also had a booth that was for our team, which I named "The Overcomers". At the booth, we had a letterbox where people could drop in their prayer request if they were wanting someone to pray for their loved one who was battling cancer. We received several requests and were able to pray for these people.

Since that time, I have also done walks for the Mito Foundation because a friend in our church has a son with Mitochondrial disease – a debilitating disease with no cure. A colleague of mine at work at the university also has a daughter with Mito. And again, I was trying to think, how can I show them support more than I am already? The fundraiser that the Mito Foundation arrange is known as "The Bloody Long Walk" – a 35-kilometer walking event in which I have now participated three times. Apart from asking for donations and raising funds for this organisation, I was doing this walk to help me! It was to increase my fitness and yet, I was helping others at the same time! And because I had signed up to do it, I couldn't back out – I had made a commitment! So, it was a win-win: a win for the Mito Foundation and a win for me and my friends with children with Mito.

The first time I did this walk, I was thinking there was no way I could walk that far! A lot of people who sign up are runners, particularly marathon runners, who do it as a training run! Not me! I am not a runner – more of a plodder. I looked at the route and calculated that I could probably manage 23 kilometres which

Walking the Bloody Long Walk Townsville, 2018

## Walking for a cause

I estimated would take me about 7 hours. So, with my walking buddy Louise, we juggled cars so that we could leave a vehicle at the 23-kilometre mark and one at the start. I did manage 23 kilometres in a day, which was more than I had walked in one day for years and years. In fact, that is the furthest I have ever walked in one day in my entire life! The walk was doing something for me as well, because I had started training, walking further and further to build up my fitness so that I could do this long walk, which was in turn, a stepping stone to doing the Camino Walk. It showed me that I could walk that far in a day.

The next year I had the opportunity to do The Bloody Long Walk when I was staying in Sydney for a couple of weeks. The route there is spectacular – a coastal walk with stunning scenery. Again, I managed about 23 kilometres, which seems to be about my limit if I want to be able to walk the next day!

The Bloody Long Walk, Sydney, 2019

More recently I have participated in a 21 kilometre (half marathon) walk for The Blue Dragon Children's Foundation in Vietnam that rescues children who have been trafficked to return home where possible, or return to safe accommodation and school, or education and training for a safer future. I wanted to be able to support this organisation because I knew about the good work that they were doing ever since I had been involved with them in facilitating a social work student who did a field placement with them.

I have also completed a half marathon walk for Dementia Australia.

For a couple of years, our church hosted a High Tea as a Mother's Day event that raised funds for needs in the community. These High Teas were catered for by members of the church who generously baked and prepared a feast. Friends, families, and members of the community attended and gave donations – as little or as much as they could afford. One year we donated funds to the Red Cross Homelessness Service Hub in Townsville and one year we donated to the North Queensland Domestic Violence Resource Service. This was another way to show compassion as a church to some of the needs in the local community.

Other ways of showing compassion and some other activities I've been involved with include cooking a meal for people that are sick, visiting people who are sick in hospital, taking meals to new mums and their families as they adjust to a new baby. Another thing I've been able to do at different times is to give blood or plasma. All it takes is a bit of my time. Each donation can save three lives. I recently posted on Facebook that I had donated plasma at the Life Blood Centre in Townsville, wanting to encourage others to give plasma if they are able. I received a message from a friend who was so thankful, as she had a family member who had needed several transfusions of plasma and didn't know who to thank – so now she thanked me! It was very humbling.

## Walking for a cause

Blood Bank Townsville, my 50th Donation, April 2019

## **What are the barriers? What stops us from showing compassion?**

Firstly, some people might say, "I don't have any special skills or abilities to help others." Well, to that I would respond with, "Do what you can do." If you're able to bake a cake, you bake that cake. If you're able to cook a pasta dish, you can take it to a neighbour or to someone who is sick. Maybe you can buy someone a coffee and "pay it forward". Are you a good listener? You can support many people just listening. Can you walk? Then you can do one of the many walkathons that support different causes.

Secondly, some people are worried that they are going to be taken advantage of or used and abused if they show kindness and compassion. It is possible that this could happen. But most often I think it is a chance we can take to bless someone else. I just think "What would Jesus do"? I find having such suspicion and seeing the worst possible view is a pessimistic approach, which is quite the opposite to how God wants us to live - by faith. God wants us to love others unconditionally, with no expectation of repayment.

Thirdly, some people have a fear of being overwhelmed. Maybe you've had an experience in the past where helping someone ended up feeling like a burden. You need to show compassion with God's strength and not do this in your own strength. Share the care with others so that you are not doing it alone. Look at what you can do, and then refer that person onto others to meet the other needs. Showing love with a smile, friendship, and acceptance costs us nothing except time. Jesus made time for everyone.

Sometimes I can feel like I have enough troubles of my own. That is when helping someone else helps me take my eyes off my problems and see that there are other people and showing a little kindness and compassion to others can mean both the other person and I can feel a little better.

## Three actions you can take as a result of reading this chapter

1. Start with a small act of kindness each week. Don't put it off until tomorrow. What can be done today? Reach out to that person who is on your heart.

2. When you hear of a need, think "can I do something about that?" Then plan and take action.

3. Encourage others to join with you. Whether you are going to give a blood donation; or whether you are going to do a walk-a-thon, share the experience with a friend or two. Whatever it is that you are doing, having the fellowship of others, makes it much easier and more fun to do.

## Additional information and resources

"A new command I give you: Love one another. As I have loved you, so you must love one another. By this everyone will know that you are my disciples, if you love one another" (John 13:34-15, New International Version).

Ephesians 2:10, says further: "We are God's handiwork created in Christ Jesus to do good works, which God prepared in advance for us to do" (New International Version).

In Ephesians 4:32: "Be kind and compassionate to one another, forgiving each other, just as in Christ God forgave you" (New International Version).

## Walking for causes

For more information on some of the causes mentioned in this chapter and others I have walked or swam for, see these websites:

https://secure.fundraising.cancer.org.au/
https://www.mito.org.au/
https://www.bluedragon.org/
https://forums.au.reachout.com/
https://www.dementia.org.au/
https://www.themay50k.org/

To give blood through The Australian Red Cross Life Blood, see https://www.donateblood.com.au/

*Chapter 10*

# Following your passion
## Reinventing yourself

You will never know if you don't have a go. I don't want to get to the end of my life and have regrets and be thinking, "I should have tried this…" or "I wonder what would have happened if I did that…" At the end of our life, it is too late.

**Why is it important to follow your passion?**

Firstly, think about how good it would be to enjoy what you spend the majority of your time on, perhaps what you do in your working day.

Secondly, following your own vision can be much more fulfilling than following someone else's dream and vision. When working for any organisation, there can be stress and conflict when the priorities and values of the employer or the business that you are working for and your own values and priorities do not align exactly.

Thirdly, when you are passionate about something, it is not a burden to put in long hours and extra effort because you are wanting to make a difference. Yet Colossians 3:23 reminds us: "Whatever you do, work at it with all your heart, as working for the Lord, not for human masters."

What is "passion"? It is an intense desire and enthusiasm for something – a fervour, zeal and eagerness.

An example in my own life was my decision to leave a permanent position at a university as a lecturer to start my own business, Interactive Solutions, as a social worker providing Supervision, Training and consultancy. This was a huge decision for me because having a permanent and regular income, of course, makes a big difference in planning one's budget and lifestyle and life. This was not something I rushed into. The timing was well considered and planned closely with my husband who was very supportive of this step of faith. I stayed on in my job at the university, reducing to part time as I started building up my business part time, providing some supervision.

I have a passion about providing good supervision for people working in the human services field, not just in social work, but also for pastors, chaplains and leaders.

Part-time, you could say that I had a foot in both camps, part of me working for the university and part for myself. I found that I felt a bit compromised, because it was hard following two different visions. Whilst I was an employee, you are bound to that organisation's vision and values and these were different to my own. I planned my resignation. I had to give six months' notice, which I did.

The freedom and fulfillment I have felt being my own boss, running my own business is extraordinary! I love being able to decide what I

## Following your passion

will say "yes" or "no" to as different contracts and work opportunities have come my way. I have been able to work to my own values and priorities. I have been able to "reinvent" myself. I have much greater flexibility with when I can take time off and have been able to prioritise making more time for family, friends and church activities. Things that are important to me!

Another example in my life has been the decision to write a book titled *Supervision and professional development in social work practice* with two colleagues, because supervision has been an area of passion in my professional life. It is the area that I did my PhD in. It seemed too good an opportunity not to publish on this area. However, I still had doubts and lacked confidence in my ability to write an academic book. My doubts were almost crippling. Fortunately, two very helpful and encouraging colleagues, Abraham Francis and Margaret -Anne Carter worked with me and we wrote the book jointly between the three of us. I was way outside of my comfort zone, but very passionate about getting information "out there". The book was published in 2019 by SAGE (see end of the chapter for more details under Additional Information and Resources).

Another example is when I applied to Chaplaincy Australia to become a registered Supervisor for pastors, chaplains and church leaders. I saw this is a way of combining the passions of my strong Christian faith and my skills as a supervisor. I thought, this is a way that I can serve church leadership at a different level in line with my professional skill and expertise. The need for support, being able to off load and debrief about many of the troubling people-issues that come to pastors and chaplains and also to reflect on what has been working well is valuable to building resilience.

A couple of months later I applied to Scripture Union Queensland to become a professional supervisor registered with them to provide similar support to school chaplains, or "chappies", in Queensland. A very similar role and for the same reasons as I had for offering to do this role for Chaplaincy Australia. I am now registered as a Supervisor with both Scripture Union and with Chaplaincy Australia.

A fourth example of following my passion has been my decision to write this book. Writing this book has taken me out of my comfort zone, but I am definitely following my passion of wanting to share my Christian faith and how living by faith is fantastic!

## Possible objections

You may want to follow your passion, but you are thinking "I can't leave my job, I have to earn an income". Well, my suggestion is that if you follow your passion part time, while working elsewhere, you can still have the regular income from your regular job and start a business on the side.

You may be thinking "but it is a risk". Yes – change and doing something new does have risks, but everything we do has risks – think of crossing a road, driving a car. There are so many risks! I decided, why not give it a try? What is the worst thing that can happen? If it doesn't work out, I can get another job.

You might then think "it's a great idea, but I'll try it later". But later never comes. You do need to think about the timing. However, you want your life to matter, to live what you are born to do, to follow your passion and you do not want to have regrets when you get to the end of your life.

## Three actions you can take as a result of reading this chapter

1. Consider what is your purpose and passion and take steps to do that.

2. What is holding you back from a decision to move or change or take a step of faith?

3. Consider what is the worst thing that could happen if you do move, change, and take a step of faith?

## Additional information and resources

"We know that in all things God works for good with those who love him, those whom he has called according to his purpose" (Romans 8:28, Good News Translation). And in The Message Translation, the verse reads, "That's why we can be sure that every detail in our lives of love for God is worked into something good."

The book I referred to earlier in this chapter:
Amanda M Nickson, Margaret-Anne Carter and Abraham P. Francis (2019) *Supervision and Professional Development in Social Work Practice*, New Delhi, India; Sage

*Chapter 11*

# Gratitude
## Changing your focus and thinking

Having gratitude changed my life at a very difficult time. During one of the most challenging periods of my life I kept a gratitude journal.

Why embrace gratitude?

How does gratitude change things?

1. Gratitude changes our focus from the problems in life to focusing on what blessings we already have.
2. We are reminded of how God has already provided for so many of our needs and of His faithfulness to us.
3. Gratitude changes our thinking. When we change our thinking, that then changes our behaviours.
4. Gratitude fills us with hope and replaces pessimism with optimism.

5. Gratitude helps us to have peace and to know that all will be well. It helps us to have a different perspective on what is going on in our lives.
6. The Bible commands us to give thanks!

In 1 Thessalonians 5:18 it says: "In everything give thanks" (New King James Version), and "be cheerful no matter what; thank God no matter what happens. This is the way God wants you who belong to Christ to live" (The Message Translation). Psalm 9:11 reads: "I will give thanks to you, Lord. With all my heart. I will tell of all your wonderful deeds" (New International Version).

What does it mean to give thanks? "Thanks" is an expression of gratitude; appreciation; acknowledgement and recognition. To be thankful is to be pleased and relieved, glad and grateful.

And what is gratitude? It is the quality of being thankful; a readiness to show appreciation for and to return kindness.

## Examples of gratitude

An example in my life is the time when I made a conscious decision to keep a gratitude diary during one of the hardest periods of my life. This was when one of my children, my eldest daughter, a young adult, was struggling with serious mental health issues. As a mother observing this and feeling helpless to do anything about the situation, it was a very difficult time. I consciously decided to keep a gratitude diary. I made a commitment to write down three things every day that I was grateful for, for a year.

I had not kept a gratitude journal such as this before. I had occasionally written down something I was thankful for, such as

## Gratitude

when I had an answered prayer. This was different – it was giving thanks in spite of my current situation and circumstances. It started off easy enough. I was able to cover the first few days easily – I was thankful to be alive, grateful to have a house, to have a roof over my head, to have access to good medical care, to have some work and income to meet my needs. Then I would have to search a little deeper – I was thankful that I had food in the pantry, that I have a fridge, that I have electricity, that I have a car that I can drive to the shops. As the days and weeks went on, I noticed a shift in my thinking. Looking around me, I could see all the provision and blessings from God over time! God had given me my faith, my church family, the ability to gather to worship freely in a church in this country. I could read and write – I had been given the gift of literacy that many other people across the world do not have.

Yet some days, those hard days, it was more of a struggle to find three more things that I was grateful for. Sometimes it would be late at night and I would be about to go to bed, and I would think, oh, I have to fill out that gratitude journal! And when you have had a day with a lot of struggles and worries and fears, such as I did on many days, when I had very difficult days with my daughter, it was harder to think of those things I was grateful for. But I persevered. And then I would think and be reminded of something beautiful in God's creation. Then I could record in my journal "Thank you for the beautiful moonlight, for the stars, for the trees and shrubs in my garden. For so many different shades of green. For clean air to breathe, for butterflies, for the sunbirds at my window each morning."

Thank you for the blue sky. Thank you for the rain. Thank you for the colours of the sunrise. I kept that journal for the year and realised, over a year, that is 365 days, I had come up with not just 1095 things I was grateful for, but that God had changed my thinking and focus to what He has done and provided in the past, and how His provision was all around me. It changed my doubts and fears about the current situation to knowing that God had everything in His hands, and it would all be okay in His timing.

Through the process of thinking what was I grateful for, I was reminded of all that God has done for the world that He has created and loves. I am able to live and breathe because of Him. His provision is all around me. And that really transformed my thoughts from focusing on the negative, on more worry and the fears for the future, those "what if's" to knowing, without a shadow of doubt, that God loves me and my family, in fact, all mankind and He has this situation covered. I could then live by faith to help my daughter one day at a time, reminded of what Jesus has done for me.

The process of keeping a gratitude journal gave me a different perspective. It reminded me that God is with us. If we struggle with things, that does not change who God is. He is faithful, and He is someone whose character can be trusted.

## Objections! What if...

You might be thinking "You don't know my life! How can I be grateful for anything? I can't think of anything." Well, I'm sure you can. You are alive today, for starters! You are breathing and you have opened your eyes for another day! Be grateful that you are alive!

You might be wondering what will happen if things get worse. Remember that God is faithful. No matter what, in every situation, you can rely on God. What if today, just for one day, you think of three things you are grateful for? See if that changes your perspective, your focus. When you are in pain, it changes your perspective, and it creates a new habit of seeing things through different eyes.

## Three actions you can take as a result of reading this chapter

1. Keep a gratitude journal for a year and record three things you are grateful for every day.

2. Thank others who have encouraged you or helped you in your life. Send them a card or letter.

3. Acknowledge God's provision and faithfulness in your life. Thank God.

**Additional information and resources**

"Lord with all my heart I thank you. I will sing your praises before the armies of angels. I face your Temple as I worship, giving thanks to you for all your loving- kindness and your faithfulness, for your promises are backed by all the honour of your name. When I pray, you answer me and encourage me by giving me the strength I need." (Psalm 138:1-3, Living Bible)

"You can pass through his open gates with the password of praise. Come right into his presence with thanksgiving. Come bring your thanks offering to him and affectionately bless his beautiful name! For the Lord is always good and ready to receive you. He's so loving that it will amaze you— so kind that it will astound you! And he is famous for his faithfulness toward all. Everyone knows our God can be trusted, for he keeps his promises to every generation!" (Psalm 100:4-5, The Passion Translation).

Look at verses in the Bible that talk about giving thanks and praise to God, being thankful. Speaking aloud the scriptures on thanksgiving is powerful and can change our thoughts and focus to God. You can search the scriptures by topic at:

https://www.biblegateway.com/

## Chapter 12

# Future focus

## Asking God, what is the next step of faith?

If you could do anything, anything at all, what would you do?

Why is it that you stay in your comfort zone, sometimes doing a job that you don't really like when you are thinking, really, I'd like to be doing something else?

Why do we need to be brave and bold and take a chance – a step of faith? What are the benefits?

You need to plan ahead if you want to change.

There is a saying that "if you change nothing, nothing changes." How can we expect change if we keep doing the same things?

Change can bring greater fulfillment and satisfaction if you are stepping into doing something that is your passion and closer to your heart's desire. Sometimes this involves taking steps of faith into the uncertain and scary unknown.

Taking action gets you started and moving. This is where results happen – after action. You may actually be able to live the life that you had always longed to live and hadn't even realised that it was possible.

Another great saying is "a goal without a plan is just a dream". How true is that! If you have always worked in one field and know deep down, you have always wanted to work in another area, to get there you need a plan in place. It might start with researching what training and qualifications you would need. Can you study that part time while continuing to work where you are? What steps would you need to take to get some work or industry experience in this area? Are there any mentors in this field you could contact? Make a plan and take the first steps towards the new you!

You will never know if you could have done something or been something or someone if you have never given it a try. Do not settle with being mediocre - be extraordinary!

What is the future for you? The future is time yet to come - time ahead of us all. Our focus is the centre of interest or activity; or an act of concentrating interest or activity on something.

So, if you want to have a future focus that is different to where you are now, whether that is in terms of work, or career, or relationships, or health and fitness, or faith, or in ministry or in how you serve others, you need to do something about it. It will not just happen magically without you taking action.

## Future focus

An example in my own life of taking action to change my future focus is writing this book, *Living by Faith*. The thought of writing this book had been on my mind for quite some time. Some people had said to me, to encourage me, "You should write a book", particularly about my experiences on Hinchinbrook Island and God's protection of me. It would be an opportunity to share what God had done in my life and to give Him the glory. However, writing about myself, and sharing experiences and stories from my own life is a long way out of my comfort zone!

I had been thinking about writing a book, but for a long time I was at that stage where I had it as a vague goal, more of a dream, but I had no plan. Then I decided I really wanted to get this book done this year. It wasn't until I made that decision, to make it a priority and put time aside, that writing the book actually happened. I had to take action, make plans in my schedule to make time to do the preparation and then the writing and make it happen. No one else could do it for me.

I have had a fantastic career as a social worker, and I am very passionate about the profession of social work and its commitment to social justice and human rights. These fit so well with my Christian values. However, deep down, I wanted to do more with my Christian faith. This has caused me to take a big step of faith in writing a book about my Christian faith and making the time to spend on this project.

My future focus includes me wanting to engage in future speaking and ministry opportunities, encouraging people in their life and faith journeys. And this is where I would like a lot of my future time to be, encouraging others in their faith. I have needed to change priorities in my life to make myself available to do this.

*Living by Faith*

**Possible objections and what if's...**

You might be thinking "I can't afford it. I can't afford to stop doing what I'm doing now". Well, I suggest just take the first step and then the next step. Make a plan, break it down into small, do-able steps, and you will get there one step at a time.

You might say, "I am not sure what my next and future focus will be?" Pray about it. Seek the counsel and advice of trusted others. Ask God to direct you.

## Three actions you can take as a result of reading this chapter

1. Dream big! Then make a plan of where you would like to be or what you would like to be doing.

2. Next, take the first step into this future that you are wanting to head towards.

3. Do some research into what it means, what you need to do to get where you want to be. For example, if you need a qualification, research what courses could get you there to be in the place you want to be.

Remember, God makes the impossible become possible! Believe for divine appointments with the right people at the right time for you.

Future focus

## Additional information and resources

Consider the use of SMART goals. SMART is a well-established tool that you can use to plan and achieve your goals. While there are a number of interpretations of the acronym's meaning, the most common one is that goals should be Specific, Measurable, Achievable, Relevant, and Time-bound. More information is available at: https://www.mindtools.com/pages/article/smart-goals.htm

# Afterword

Congratulations on reading *Living by Faith*! Are you ready to put this into action?

Do you know Jesus Christ as your personal Lord and Saviour? Are you ready now to make things right between you and God? The Bible teaches that "All have sinned and fall short of the glory of God" (Romans 3:23, New International Version). Sin is simply our separation from God. Romans 6:23 states that: "The wages of sin is death, but the gift of God is eternal life in Christ Jesus." Jesus has made a way for us to be able to restore our relationship with God.

John 11:25-26 says: "Jesus said to her, 'I am the resurrection and the life. The one who believes in me will live, even though they die; and whoever lives by believing in me will never die. Do you believe this?'" (New International Version).

If you would like to have a new life, with Jesus as your Lord and Saviour, it is as simple as having this conversation, and speaking directly with God. You can repeat these words, or say something similar:

*"Thank you, Lord Jesus, that you died for my sins. Forgive me for all I have done wrong and for not having you as the Lord of my life. I accept you now, Jesus, as my Lord and Saviour. Help me to follow you and live for you. Amen."*

Congratulations! You have restored your relationship with God.

To build your faith, remember some of the keys in this book:

- Spending time getting to know the Bible and reading, studying, and learning some of the scripture.
- Spending regular time in prayer. This is having a conversation with God – He wants to have a close relationship with you.
- Finding people who can encourage you in your faith and you encouraging them. This could include finding a local church that you can be part of. Look for a church that is friendly and helps you to grow in faith with good teaching.
- Practicing gratitude. Try a 30 day gratitude challenge – keep a journal and write down three things you are grateful for each day for 30 days
- Look after yourself – find ways to replenish your body, mind, emotions and spirit. This is important!
- Show compassion to others.
- Ask God to guide you in what your next steps of faith are.

More resources to help you in your journey of faith are available on the website:
http://www.amandanickson.com.au/

# About The Author

Dr. Amanda Nickson is a wife, a mother, a social worker and a Christian.

She grew up in Sydney with her parents, until their separation when she was 17, and her younger sister. She spent her childhood enjoying many activities including playing the piano, singing in choirs, playing chamber music and in orchestras, and tennis. After she finished school, Amanda went to the University of New South Wales to study Social Work. At the time, she was actively involved in her local church youth group, volunteered for beach missions, and enjoyed bushwalking. She started working in social work in western Sydney before moving to Central Queensland.

Amanda chose social work as her profession as an extension of her Christian faith, being able to help and serve others at their point of need. She has worked in a variety of positions in government, non-government organisations, academia and private practice across a range of fields: community development, individual and family work, group work, community education, covering issues as diverse as child protection, juvenile justice, adoptions, health, defence, homelessness, domestic violence, finance and refugees. She lectured in social work for 13 years at James Cook University in Townsville. Currently, Amanda runs her own business, Interactive Solutions (www.interactivesolutions.org.au) in training, supervision, social work services and organisational consultancy.

Amanda has a PhD in Social Work and is recognised in her field as an expert in social work supervision. Whilst an accomplished professional and public speaker, in this book Amanda focuses on her first love and passion, her Christian faith, and how living by faith is at the core of everything she does.

Amanda has been a Christian for over 40 years and has served as a leader in various positions in her local church. She is a registered Supervisor with Chaplaincy Australia and with Scripture Union, Queensland. Her passion is to encourage others in their journey of faith and to help bring people to a closer personal relationship with God.

Amanda now lives in Townsville with her husband, two of her three adult children, her dog Jaffa and her cat Kitty. She loves nothing more than catching up with friends with a cup of tea, especially a Devonshire tea or high tea, and making time to walk in nature, such as in the beautiful national parks close to home and further afield.

# Acknowledgements

I am thrilled that the idea of this book has become a reality and I hope that it brings great encouragement to all readers.

First, I would like to acknowledge God and thank Him for all He has done in my life and all He has brought me through. With God, all things are possible. The gift of faith in Jesus Christ is life-changing - it brings hope. I appreciate, and would like to thank and acknowledge, the influence and gift of time and encouragement of many Christian pastors, leaders, and fellow believers in my life in many different places who have all helped me to grow in faith.

I especially want to acknowledge the love and support of my family who have encouraged me in this journey as an author of this book. To my husband Daryl, and my children Jessica, Danielle, and Timothy – thank you!

For my friends who have been interested and supportive of my book-writing venture, your words of encouragement have meant the world to me. I would particularly like to acknowledge and thank those men and women of faith who have generously given of their time to write a testimonial for this book. I have been truly humbled and encouraged by what you have said. Thank you from the bottom of my heart.

To the publishing and mentoring team at the Ultimate 48 Hour Author, thank you so much for your support, wisdom and guidance in the writing and publishing of this book. Your influence has made what seemed out of reach – writing this book - not only possible but also enjoyable along the way. Thank you for investing your mentoring and expertise in me.

# Speaker Bio

Dr. Amanda Nickson is the author of *Living by Faith*. With a PhD in social work and a reputation as an expert in social work supervision, Amanda is a highly regarded speaker and teacher in her professional life as a social worker.

Whilst an accomplished professional and public speaker, Amanda focuses on her first love and passion, her Christian faith and how living by faith is at the core of everything she does.

After a powerful experience that could have left her paralysed, Amanda shares her experiences in an engaging and confident way that leaves the audiences feeling connected and plugged in.

Amanda's passion is to encourage others in their journey of faith to help people develop a closer personal relationship with God.

Amanda keynotes which can be customised to suit any audience include:

- Overcoming doubt and fear to reach your full potential
- Trust and gratitude when facing impossible situations

- Self compassion, compassion and resilience
- Taking steps of faith into a new, exciting future

To enquire about booking Amanda to speak at your next event or for prices and availabilities email

amanda@amandanickson.com.au

or

amanda.nickson4@gmail.com

# Offers and call to action

**Offer 1:**

A free copy of Chapter 1 – available as a sampler as a PDF - great to share with others who may be interested. Available at http://www.amandanickson.com.au/

**Offer 2:**

*Living by Faith* 12-week course and Bible studies (online or with a study guide). See website at http://www.amandanickson.com.au/ for details. Mention this offer for a 30% discount.

**Offer 3:**

Engage Dr. Amanda Nickson as a speaker for you next event, women's meeting, youth meetings.

Amanda's keynotes which can be customised to suit any audience include:

*Living by Faith*

- Overcoming doubt and fear to reach your full potential
- Trust and gratitude when facing impossible situations
- Self compassion, compassion and resilience
- Taking Steps of Faith into a New Exciting Future

To enquire about booking Amanda to speak at your next event or for availabilities and costs email

amanda@amandanickson.com.au

## Offer 4:

View Amanda talking about her Miracle on Hinchinbrook on YouTube - https://www.youtube.com/watch?v=vclla-Q9Z9E

# Notes

www.ingramcontent.com/pod-product-compliance
Lightning Source LLC
Chambersburg PA
CBHW021154080526
44588CB00008B/328